*Jean de Reszke, the Polish tenor who first sang the role in London at Drury Lane in Italian.
He made his American debut as Lohengrin in Chicago in 1891. This photograph from the
album of Lady de Grey, doyenne of Covent Garden around 1900, is inscribed: 'the Lohengrin
"par excellence" '. (Royal Opera House Archives)*

Lohengrin

Richard Wagner

Opera Guide Series Editor: Nicholas John

John Calder · London
Riverrun Press · New York

Published in association with English National Opera

COPYRIGHT DATA

First published in Great Britain, 1993, by
Calder Publications Ltd.,
9-15 Neal Street, London WC2H 9TU

Published in the U.S.A., 1993, by
Riverrun Press Inc., 1170 Broadway,
New York, NY 10001

ISBN 0 7145 3852 3

BRITISH LIBRARY CATALOGUING IN PUBLICATION DATA

Wagner, Richard
  Lohengrin. — English National Opera guide; 47)
  I. Title   II. Holden, Amanda   III. Series
  782.1092

LIBRARY OF CONGRESS CATALOGUING IN PUBLICATION DATA *is available*

English National Opera receives financial assistance from the Arts Council of Great Britain.

Typeset in Plantin by Spooner Graphics, London NW5

Printed in Great Britain

CONTENTS

LIST OF ILLUSTRATIONS

Wagner's 'Alter Ego'

John Deathridge

The critical star of *Lohengrin* has dimmed so much over the years that even Wagner's admirers sometimes find it hard to let it shine as brightly as it did at the height of the opera's popularity in the nineteenth and early twentieth centuries. The swan, one of the opera's central symbols, has become a kitsch icon, capable of selling anything from kettles to the Queen's favourite matches, but no longer quite the beautiful, enigmatic and sexually aggressive image it used to be. Harder to accept now, too, is the gullibility of the heroine Elsa. After falling in love with Lohengrin she is bartered with her consent in a marriage transaction forbidding her even to ask his name and origin. (Lévi-Strauss has said that we no longer need to resort to the matrimonial vocabulary of Great Russia to see that in marriages like this the groom is the 'merchant' and the bride the 'merchandise' in a contract ensuring the continued existence of a male-dominated community.)

Stranger still are the medieval dualisms and theological mysteries of faith and redemption that nourish the plot of *Lohengrin*. Today they seem like distant relics, at least at first sight. But they probably looked just as odd to some observers in the context of the German idealism of the 1840s when the opera was composed. Wagner probably sensed this himself, which may be one of the reasons for his occasional metamorphosis — albeit in private — into one of the opera's earliest critics. A few months after the successful première in Weimar (which as a political refugee banned from Germany he could not attend) he wrote to the literary scholar Adolf Stahr:

> There is a whole world between *Lohengrin* and my present plans. [Wagner had just started work on *Siegfried*.] What is so terribly embarrassing for me is to see a snake-skin I shed long ago dangled in front of me willy-nilly as if I were still in it. If I could have everything my way, *Lohengrin* — the libretto of which I wrote in 1845 — would be long *forgotten* in favour of new works that prove, even to me, that I have made progress. (May 31, 1851)

Post-war generations have tended to agree. The former popularity of *Lohengrin* is suspect — fodder for the sentimental and old-fashioned perhaps, or a salutary reminder of the (supposedly) revisionist feudal ambitions of the old German middle class — while the daring modernity of Wagner's later works is admired and celebrated. During and immediately after the composition of *Lohengrin* Wagner became enraptured with Young Hegelian ideas, devoured Feuerbach's critique of Christian belief (which threw a rather different light on the Christian symbolism of the opera), turned into a ferocious orator against the old feudal order in Germany, fought on the barricades in the 1849 Dresden Revolution, more or less gave up composing to write lengthy, socially-critical tomes about the future of art, nearly jettisoned his marriage and 'domesticity' (as he put it to Stahr), and began to develop a huge work that eventually became the *Ring* in which myth and music were to combine in an utopian Artwork of the Future expressing profound insights into the world in ways no existing art form had ever done before. In other words, Wagner was telling Stahr that he had changed almost within the space of two years irreversibly into a modernist in the Young Hegelian mould who believed in correcting the mistakes of the past not by rejuvenating the old order, but by destroying it completely, and creating something radically new in its place. That hardly sounded any more like the author of *Lohengrin*.

Wagner told Stahr in a suggestive phrase of the 'twilight mist' (Dämmerdunst) lifting from him after *Lohengrin*, as if to say that he had experienced a kind of dawn banishing the dark magic and medieval miracle-worship at the centre of the opera from his mind for good. That the situation was not quite as simple as this must have been clear to Wagner, who was actually taking issue in his letter (for diplomatic reasons only implicitly) with a recently published and highly influential article on *Lohengrin* by Franz Liszt. On Wagner's behalf Liszt had prepared and conducted the opera's first performance in Weimar on the 101st anniversary of Goethe's birth (August 28 1850) and taken great pains to ensure that the place and date would be seen to be highly symbolic. A growing nostalgia in Germany after the failed revolutions of 1848/9 for Weimar's former cultural glory, together with Wagner's burgeoning reputation as the new hope of German art, inevitably focused critical attention on the production. Also, the composer's enforced absence, and his status as a political exile with a price on his head, inevitably caught the lavish attention of the liberal intelligentsia and the press. Not surprisingly the première turned out to be a major event that transformed Wagner virtually overnight from a provincial German Kapellmeister into an international figure.

Liszt's sense of timing and uncanny knack for publicity did not desert him when he introduced *Lohengrin* to the world as an administrator and conductor. But Wagner was arguably less pleased with the high-flown language of his friend's essay on the opera (written in French and first published in German translation in April 1851) which at the start conjures up an undialectical and sentimental image of a premodern world unsullied by doubt in Christian belief. That alone could have hardly found favour with a recent convert to Feuerbach and admirer of the Hegelian Left. The constant implication of Liszt's argument is that, like the knight of the Grail, the opera is a marvellous wonder sent into a world that has 'rejected miracles' and no longer 'believes in divine origin or divine revelation'. The pleasing sounds of the Prelude as if 'reflected on a broad and calm stretch of water' can help us to grasp again the 'indescribable power' of the secret of the Holy Grail. The opera shows us that what humanity needs is not yet more scientific endeavour, but an antidote to 'the hate and envy that have befallen the men of invention and progress' — a cure for a civilisation that is slowly being strangled by reason and lack of faith.

Not to be outdone, Wagner decided in 1851 to make his view of *Lohengrin* known publicly as well. In a long autobiographical essay entitled *A Communication to my Friends*, he dismissed the Christian imagery in *Lohengrin* as 'fortuitous' and argued ingeniously for a more fundamental view of the legend. He pleaded for a more critical method that could reveal what is known in modern parlance as the 'deep structure' of all myths that relate them to each other. The story of the *Flying Dutchman* is nothing less than a reincarnation of the myth of the *Odyssey*, while the image of Odysseus yearning for an earthly woman, and escaping the clutches of Calypso and the attractiveness of Circe, has found its way in 'enhanced' form into *Tannhäuser*. Likewise, the relation of a supernatural being to a mortal in the myth of Zeus and Semele clearly relates it to the story of *Lohengrin*, though here Wagner was prepared to go even further than a comparison with the Greeks:

Charles Dalmorès, the French tenor, who sang Lohengrin in 1908 at Bayreuth. (Royal Opera House Archives)

A primal feature, repeated in manifold forms, permeates the legends of those nations who dwelt by the sea or by rivers that emptied into the sea: on the billows' azure mirror a stranger was seen to draw near, a man of utmost grace and purest virtue who charmed and won each heart by the irresistible spell which he wove; he was the fulfilment of that desire which fills the yearning breast of him who dreamt of happiness beyond the sea in a land he could not discern. The stranger disappeared again, withdrawing over the ocean waves, as soon as he was questioned about his innermost being. *(Translation Stewart Spencer)*

Passages like this which reduce a complex web of tales and legends to a key image of great emotional import amply confirm Wagner's modern reputation as the 'father of the structural analysis of myth' (Lévi-Strauss). In an exhaustive study of the Lohengrin legend published in 1911, Otto Rank, a pupil and colleague of Sigmund Freud, came to the conclusion that the truly astonishing prevalence of the same symbols in so many branches of the myth must reflect, as Wagner had already suspected, primal feelings of awesome power. Indeed, Rank opened such a veritable can of psychoanalytical worms in his detailed account of the anxieties and taboos hidden behind the seemingly innocuous fairy-tale surface of *Lohengrin* that even in a post-Freudian era which has grown rather weary of the unconscious it is hard to ignore. The hero's arrival on 'the billows' is not surprisingly — at least in Freudian terms — the birth out of the waters of the mother's womb, and his departure a return into the underworld and the realm of death. The forbidden question is the code of silence imposed on the child asking after the secret of its own or its parents' origin. To pacify the child the right answer is repressed and replaced by the fantasy of the stork, or in many regions and countries the white swan, which pulls the new-born child out of the water in a casket, and brings it to its parents as if by a miracle.

Rank also came to the conclusion that the forbidden question serves to hide an incestuous relationship which is revealed and therefore proscribed the moment the identity of the hero is known. The inevitable comparison with the Oedipus myth turns *Lohengrin* in this scenario into a 'rescue fantasy' about the hero's 'mother' that ends in her death. (The strange coincidence that Wagner's mother died when *Lohengrin* was just on the verge of completion did not go unnoticed by Rank.) Here Rank drew on Freud's theory of the injured third party which suggests that some men develop an unconscious need to save their mothers from the threat of the rival father, and in order to relive the fantasy are instinctively drawn to women already attached to other men. (Rank was also not slow to point out that Wagner's famous adulterous love affairs, and the similar triangle situations in all his stage works from *The Flying Dutchman* to *Parsifal*, follow a similar behavioural pattern.

Friedrich von Telramund has formally renounced his claim on Elsa before *Lohengrin* begins. But Rank had little trouble in showing that the attachment is still strong enough for Telramund to function, psychoanalytically speaking, as the evil father whom Lohengrin has to confront in order to save his surrogate mother Elsa. Wagner took pains to change the sequence of events in the various versions of the legend in order to allow this traumatic confrontation to recur with increasing intensity, as in certain kinds of dream that repeat a single theme in different contexts with greater clarity each time. Lohengrin easily wins his battle with

10

Margit Angerer, the Hungarian soprano, as Elsa (Royal Opera House Archives)

Anja Silja as Ortrud in the production by Robert Wilson and Susanne Raschig, Zurich, 1991 (photo: Schlegel and Edle)

Telramund on Elsa's behalf in the first act. But in the second he intervenes only just in time in a far more fraught situation between Elsa and Telramund as Elsa's doubts about the forbidden question begin to surface. After Elsa decides on her wedding night in the third act to break the code of silence and to ask the question, Lohengrin kills Telramund at last, finally revealing his identity and origin in the concluding tableau over the dead body of his 'father', and hence also the real nature of the 'incest' with the woman he set out to rescue.

Wagner's prescient insight into the nature of myth allowed him to see *Lohengrin* in 1851 paradoxically as a thoroughly modern work pointing to a utopian future precisely because it returns to the most fundamental origins of human feeling. Liszt was right nonetheless to stress the opera's culturally more specific traits, such as its obvious Christian symbolism and celebration of the medieval past, which Wagner's modernist posture at the time tended to obscure. (Rank dutifully follows Wagner, incidentally, in practically ignoring them too.) The final scene alone is liberally provided with Christian motifs. The dove which appears above Lohengrin's boat to pull it away when he withdraws over the ocean is an image that has strong association with the Immaculate Conception. As the power of Lohengrin's prayer returns the swan to its original human form, a pagan symbol of miraculous birth is replaced by a specifically Christian one. Indeed, the very notion of the swan as a human being whose outer shape has been tragically altered touches on the idea central to Christian doctrine that only body and soul together can define an individual, and that rending the two asunder is the most terrible prospect anyone can face. Elsa is not only punished for answering the forbidden question by her parting from Lohengrin, whose true identity she has only just discovered, but also by the separation of her soul from her body before she slowly slips lifeless to the ground. (In the stage direction describing the death of Elsa Wagner uses the poetic expression *entseelt*, which in the context can be taken to mean literally 'deprived of a soul'.)

Wagner was never one to scoff at medieval superstition. Nor did he necessarily disagree in private with friends like Liszt, who were still sympathetic in the early 1850s to the idea that whole areas of subjective feeling and religious belief are not susceptible to philosophical enquiry and grandiose modern programmes about the social function of art. The terrifying symbolism which caught the imagination of the medieval mind, no matter how primitive or irrational it was, had continued to affect believers at all levels of society, and could not simply be brushed neatly and tidily under a thick intellectual carpet called the Artwork of the Future. This may be the reason why in the manuscript full score of *Lohengrin* Wagner privately dedicated it to Liszt with the enigmatic words 'to his "alter ego" ', but not in the printed edition where the wording is more bland. As the bright new star of German music and respected by the Young Hegelian Left, he was not yet ready to concede in public (though he did much later after absorbing Schopenhauer) that beneath the enchanting surface and ethereal colours of *Lohengrin* there is a darker level where utopian visions of the future quickly pale before deep-seated fears which have to be addressed if real social change is to take place.

Lauritz Melchior as Lohengrin at Covent Garden in 1935 (Royal Opera House Archives)

Wagner's 'Lohengrin': between grand opéra and Musikdrama

Thomas S. Grey

I
'Lohengrin' and the ambivalent legacy of *grand opéra*

Many of the things Wagner vehemently abjured in public he continued to consort with privately throughout his life: the French and the Jews, for instance, the symphonic genre (declared dead, though he secretly hoped to resurrect it after *Parsifal*), or the music of Mendelssohn (selectively admitted into the canon of Bayreuth *Hausmusik*). Similar contradictions mark his attitudes towards *grand opéra*. Wagner had ostensibly rejected the genre after *Rienzi* (1839-41), his own *grand opéra* with a German text, and he excoriated its leading exponent, Giacomo Meyerbeer — both by innuendo in 'Judaism in Music', and by name in *Opera and Drama*. Yet nearly all his operas and music dramas owe something to French grand opera as practised by Auber, Halévy and Meyerbeer, especially with regard to their musical dramaturgy: the calculated disposition of characters and musical material over large expanses (lyrical monologues, dramatic dialogues, grandiose ensemble-choral tableaux) and, above all, the taste for either cataclysmic or transcendental endings.[1]

The ambivalent legacy of *grand opéra* is particularly evident in the last two 'Romantic operas' — *Tannhäuser* and *Lohengrin* — that precede Wagner's exile from Germany and the momentous transition to a new genre of 'music drama' after 1850. Though composed after his physical and spiritual return to Saxony in 1840, they would not have turned out as they did without the musical and theatrical experiences of two and a half years in Paris. Even before embarking on his Parisian expedition Wagner had loudly proclaimed (as loudly as was possible for a still unknown composer) the need to submit the provincial operatic styles of Weber, Spohr, Marschner and their followers to the cosmopolitan sophistication of French grand opera as well as to the vocal refinement of Bellinian *bel canto*. But then, upon leaving Paris in a mood of defeat and degradation, Wagner turned rapidly (and rabidly) against French opera, as epitomized by Meyerbeer's commercial success in *Robert le diable* and *Les Huguenots*. Despite this apparent change of tune, *Tannhäuser* and *Lohengrin* in many ways fulfil the rapprochement between German Romantic opera and French (or Franco-Italian) grand opera that Wagner had earlier promoted as the way of the future.[2]

Lohengrin becomes a particularly interesting case study of Wagnerian ambivalence due to its position on the brink of Wagner's private aesthetic

---

1 Dahlhaus states that '*Lohengrin* is a grand opera. [It] can in fact be construed as the perfected manifestation of a pattern developed by Scribe and Meyerbeer in which affairs of state grow out of private actions and, in an exact dramaturgical analogy, large-scale choral and ensemble scenes evolve from arias and duets.' ('Wagner's Place in the History of Music', *Wagner Handbook*, ed. Müller & Wapnewski; Harvard, 1992).

2 See 'Die deutsche Oper' (1834), 'Halévy und die französische Oper'(1842), and especially 'Über Meyerbeers "Huguenotten"', *Sämtliche Schriften und Dichtungen* (Leipzig, 1911-16, vol.12). The genesis of the posthumously published Meyerbeer essay remains unclear. See Döhring in *Wagnerliteratur-Wagnerforschung* ed. Dahlhaus & Voss (Mainz, 1985), and Weinland in *Richard Wagner zwischen Beethoven und Schönberg* (*Musik-Konzepte*, vol. 59: Munich, 1988).

revolution, which coincided with the political upheavals of 1848-49 and with the early genesis of *Der Ring des Nibelungen*. During the time *Lohengrin* was conceived and executed, between 1845 and 1848, Wagner steeped himself in the mythologies of Ancient Greece and pre-Christian Europe, as well as in their literary legacy in classical tragedy, Norse saga and medieval Germanic epic. From all this, and from the medieval sources for *Tannhäuser* and *Lohengrin*, he developed a vision of an authentic, 'purely human' dramatic *Gesamtkunstwerk* (total art-work) whose ambitions far outstripped those of any of his earlier programmes of operatic reform. This was nothing less than a programme of universal social and cultural regeneration (from which he never retreated, despite his subsequent political disillusionments). Its ultimate significance was to transcend such practical goals as naturally expressive vocal declamation, the eradication of 'absolute' musical form inherited from an age of political absolutism and aesthetic artifice, or the separation of musical-scenic 'effect' from dramatically motivated action. The works Wagner conceived during this period of intellectual ferment (*Lohengrin* and to a certain extent *Siegfrieds Tod*, the original version of *Götterdämmerung*) bear the marks of a creative dilemma: while Wagner was speculating about a new kind of dramatic musical art-work informed by the human content of myth, the only viable model was *grand opéra*. The vehemence of his polemics against opera (and especially against contemporary French opera) in *Opera and Drama* is partly a result of his frustration in realizing his ambitions, and his initial inability to develop a suitable musical language for his Siegfried drama.

By the time of *Lohengrin*, Wagner had made every effort to divest himself of the trappings of the more superficial side of *grand opéra*, especially the military choruses and vacuous ballets (such as he had mimicked in *Rienzi*). What he retained, however, were large-scale models of operatic dramaturgy, which he imbued with an increasingly original musical voice, even if this voice has a timbre we now recognize as a kind of awkward adolescent break.

Grand ensemble tableaux were the hallmark of *grand opéra* in the 1830s and '40s, and *Lohengrin* clearly reveals its debt to this tradition. It is dominated by public scenes: the chorus and public figures (Henry the Fowler, nobles, the herald, pages, ladies-in-waiting, and so on) are present throughout the first act, in three of the five scenes of Act Two, and in the first and third scenes of Act Three — for roughly two-thirds of the opera. The concluding portions of Acts One and Two bear the strongest imprint of grand operatic dramaturgy in the pageantry which forms a backdrop for *coups-de-théâtre*, such as Lohengrin's arrival and the trial-by-combat, or the interruption of Elsa's procession to the Minster and Elsa's resolve not to pose the 'forbidden question' to Lohengrin in Act Two.

The interrupted ceremonial procession was one of the most reliable dramaturgical devices of *grand opéra*. Act Two not only has obvious precedents but also provided a model for later composers who otherwise remained oblivious to Wagner's music. Prominent examples with which Wagner was familiar include Act One of Auber's *La muette de Portici* (1828) — when the mute girl Fenella disrupts the nuptials of her seducer, Alfonso — and Act Two of Halévy's *La juive* (1835), where another ceremonial involving a betrothed noble couple (Eudoxie and Léopolde) is disrupted when the powerless heroine (Rachel) recognises Léopolde as her unknown lover. Halévy's *Reine de Chypre* (1841), which Wagner reviewed for both French and German papers and arranged in piano-vocal score for the Paris

Gösta Winbergh as Lohengrin in the production by Robert Wilson and Susanne Raschig, Zurich, 1991 (photo: Schlegel and Edle)

publisher Schlesinger, contains no less than two interrupted nuptials: in the first act, the wedding of the protagonist (Caterina Cornaro) to her original fiancé and true love, Gérard de Courcy, is thwarted by the machinations of the Venetian oligarchy; several acts later the celebration of Caterina's politically arranged marriage to the French ruler of Cyprus is cut short by Gérard in turn bent on revenge. (The most celebrated instance of the scenario, the coronation scene in Meyerbeer's *Le prophète* and its interruption when Fidès recognises the false prophet as her son, was not staged until after Wagner had completed *Lohengrin*, although its origins go back to the time of his early Paris years.)

While Scribe's *coup-de-théâtre* in *Le prophète* is more theatrically effective than the interruptions of Elsa's bridal train, Wagner's musical realization is more broadly conceived. In the ensemble that forms the climax of Act Two, Wagner has created one of the finest examples of that purely operatic type: the moment of tension, suspense or shock that serves to motivate a tableau in which the conflicting emotions of the principals are woven together against a background of choral commentary and atmospheric accompaniment. The ensemble impresses in a number of ways. Foremost is the sheer intricacy and variety of the combined solo and choral lines. The solo writing simultaneously expresses conflicting emotions, while the choral writing is distinguished by a quasi-naturalistic variety of pacing and texture, such as Wagner advocated in *Opera and Drama* (the idea that Wagner rejects the use of chorus here is a popularly-held misapprehension). Elsa's lines, in particular, are clearly projected above the ensemble, distinguished from the rest by width of overall range, as well as by the fact that she follows the top line of the texture (the separateness of her vocal line thus also embodies the stage direction — that Elsa should be 'staring straight ahead, oblivious to her surroundings'). Ortrud's and Friedrich's lines occasionally merge with the sinister and sinuous diminished-seventh contours of Ortrud's characteristic motif [15] in the orchestra, without being strictly bound to it. Lohengrin twice injects a nobly arching figure in C major, begging heaven to strengthen Elsa's resolve ('O Himmel! Schirme sie vor den Gefahren!' 'O Heaven! Shelter her from this great danger!'), while the King voices his moral support in a firm diatonic bass line (see example 1a). Despite the infamous metrical stolidity characteristic of the *Lohengrin* score (which might be defended as a feature of what Verdians would call its *tinta*, its legendary chivalric milieu), Wagner subtly nuances the chorus declamation. Compare, for example, the hesitant rhythms of the men's voices that begin the ensemble ('Welch ein Gehimniss' 'What is the secret') in B flat with the simple rhythms and stalwart down-beats in which they subsequently voice their support for Lohengrin ('Wir schirmen ihn, den Edlen, vor Gefahren' 'We will protect this hero from all danger') in C major (see examples 1b and 1c). While the minor-major harmonic plan of the ensemble (C minor to C major) is typical of such concerted tableaux, Wagner enriches this basic trajectory. The initial C minor area is coloured by the diminished-seventh sounds of Ortrud's motif, for example, and the initial move into C major (at Elsa's words 'die er errettet, weh' mir Undankbaren!' 'but he has saved me. How could I betray him?') overshoots the immediate goal, moving out towards E minor before returning to C, through an augmented-sixth progression, at Lohengrin's phrase shown in example 1a ('Oh Himmel! Schirme sie' 'O Heaven! Shelter her'). Furthermore this C major is only temporary, and returns circuitously to C

Example 1a
Andante moderato/Mäßig langsam

19

minor through Ortrud-based diminished harmonies; the whole concludes with an ominous cadence (F minor to C) generated by the motif of the 'forbidden question' [12], ringing out in the full orchestra as the characters variously contemplate the consequences of asking it (Elsa: 'Wüsst' ich sein Loos! 'Ah, if I knew'; Ortrud and Freidrich: 'Er is besiegt, wird ihm die Frage kund!' 'he will be lost, lost if his name is known!'). This anticipates the end of Act Two, where the same motif, at the same pitch, accompanies Ortrud's defiant gesture, casting a fateful shadow over the brilliant C major close of the act.

The effect of all this is heightened by its position within the second, 'public' portion of Act Two. The three scenes encompass a single ceremony: Elsa's progress to the Minster. The initial disruption of the procession by Ortrud (cutting off the cadence of the large opening chorus in E flat) leads to a lengthy altercation between the two women — with chorus — which is not resolved but pre-empted by the appearance of Lohengrin and the King and a large-scale shift to C major. The procession recommences in C major, at which point Friedrich launches a parallel cadential disruption and a parallel altercation ensues. Thus the frozen-

Example 1b

Mäßig langsam

Example 1c

action ensemble represents the culmination of a process of intensification (procession-interruption-altercation, twice over), and the procession reaches its goal only after recommencing a third time, now recalling the original music of Elsa's *Brautgang* [20]. The final structural cadence specifically completes the musical gesture that had been cut short by Ortrud several hundred bars before, now transposed from E flat to C. Wagner learned to deploy such large gestures from the repertory of French grand opera but he often applied them to musical designs of greater sophistication and integrity. Of course the dichotomy of 'theatrical' versus 'musical' or 'symphonic' can just as easily be invoked to condemn Wagner as to praise him (following Nietzsche's example). In the final analysis, the concluding scenes of Act Two remain more theatrically 'effective' than symphonically 'cohesive'. When compared with their prototypes, however, Wagner's scenes are distinguished by the continuous evolution which would constitute an essential factor in his subsequent ideal of 'music drama'.

The third and final scene of Act One — Lohengrin's arrival and defence of Elsa — is similarly structured around a conventional operatic core, although here the disparity between novelty and convention is even more strongly projected than in Act Two. The operatic core consists of a Germanic version of the standard Italianate ensemble-prayer (including *a cappella* passages) and a fast, stretta-like conclusion ('O fänd' ich Jubelweisen, deinen Ruhme gleich' 'Oh, could I find the words to celebrate and raise'). Wagner admitted he had conceived the opening solo paragraph independently of the text (that is, in the manner of the 'absolute' operatic melody he condemned so harshly in *Opera and Drama*), and even confessed that it might be influenced by Spontini.[3] Both prayer and finale, however, are infused with restless modulatory passages which raise the musical temperature of even these more conventional numbers, at the same time lending them a recognisable Wagnerian stamp.

The choral response to Lohengrin's miraculous arrival (bridging scenes 2 and 3) is among the score's most novel moments, on the other hand, demonstrating the kind of thing Wagner must have had in mind when he called in *Opera and Drama*, Part III, for a new treatment of the chorus as a collection of individuals rather than as a homogeneous harmonic backdrop. Across the first full statement of Lohengrin's identifying motif [8] an eight-part chorus gradually coalesces out of fragmentary ejaculations of wonder and surprise, emerging into regular block-chordal homophony only at the moment when the hero's peculiar vessel reaches the shore. A complementary tone of hushed awe is struck in the next chorus, following Lohengrin's arioso farewell to the swan [10]. The harmonically conceived polyphony of this second chorus ('Wie fasst uns selig süsses Grauen' 'What sense of wonder overcomes us!' [11]) is reminiscent of the textures of the Prelude, a connection that is reinforced by the citation of the Prelude's opening bars at the beginning of Lohengrin's 'farewell' and by the key of A major. The style of both this chorus and the Prelude reminds us that Wagner construed the polyphony of Palestrina and his era primarily as a freely 'floating', metrically unfettered, exploration of harmonic sonorities, and only secondarily as counterpoint. Thus the conscious evocation of a

---

3 See Deathridge, 'Through the Looking-Glass: Some Remarks on the First Complete Draft of *Lohengrin*', in *Analysing Opera: Verdi and Wagner*, ed. Abbate & Parker (Berkeley and Los Angeles, 1989). On the latter point, see *Cosima Wagner's Diaries*, vol. 2 (p. 252), ed. Gregor-Dellin & Mack, tr. Skelton (New York, 1979).

sacred, 'Christian' tone in Wagner's music here, as later in *Parsifal*, eschews imitative counterpoint — the traditional music of religious sentiments, like the chorale — in favour of a shimmering harmonic tissue of semi-independent lines.[4]

Wagner's most famous music (apart from the 'Ride of the Valkyries') is the so-called Wedding March [24] and it occurs in a scene given over entirely to stage ceremony and empty of all individual utterance or action. (The context of Act Three makes the title doubly inappropriate: the music's function is to accompany the now-married couple to their bridal suite, where the marriage will be dissolved within less than twenty-four hours.) In reducing the brief scene to ceremonial Wagner has taken an opposite tack towards the conventions of *grand opéra* from his expansion of them elsewhere. Such ceremonial scenes typically involve the expression of private emotions — often doubt or consternation — in solo asides. Wagner instead reserves the private conflict for a lengthy dialogue scene in which Elsa's misgivings are gradually and more 'organically' developed. The opening scene becomes almost a second entracte, following the festive Prelude. His use of the offstage band creates — in its intermingling with the pit orchestra and through the aural image of the arrival and departure of the procession — a subtle parallel to the Act One Prelude as an allegory of Lohengrin's role. Sounds approach from offstage (chorus and wind-band with harps and a discreet triangle); as the chorus enters with Elsa and Lohengrin, the music is 'grounded' in the pit orchestra, with fuller winds and a light addition of strings. While Elsa and Lohengrin remain on stage, the chorus and processional music retreat, and the strains of flute, harp and higher voices evaporate, like the Grail music at the end of the Prelude, where the gesture anticipates Lohengrin's eventual departure for the zone from whence he materialized.

The canonization of this music in later Victorian times as 'the' wedding march, alongside Mendelssohn's (an unlikely consort!), suggests the appeal of *Lohengrin* to a bourgeois sensibility, to which both its musical idiom and dramatic message seem better suited than those of any other Wagner stage work. Here and elsewhere, the soft-edged woodwind timbres (like tones of a sweetly registrated organ or harmonium) envelop Elsa like the white folds of her wedding garments. Lohengrin's motif, first heard in the same timbre when Elsa recounts her vision of him in Act One but subsequently entrusted to trumpets or full orchestra, seems to have distilled from the military-band marches of Spontini or Halévy — or *Rienzi* — a bourgeois sound ideal of masculine rectitude as the essence of knightly virtue. This transformation has to do in part with a retreat from the pedestrian, four-square march tunes of *grand opéra* towards a more pliable motivic substance, but also with a new range of timbres.

4 The sequence of events in this and the preceding scene closely resembles the third-act finale of Marschner's *Templer und Jüdin* (1829, after Scott's *Ivanhoe*), where the falsely accused Jewess, Rebecca, waits helplessly for a heaven-sent champion (*Kämpe*) to step forward in her defence. All the dramaturgical and even musical elements of Wagner's scene are present: the Herald's fanfare-summons, the heroine's prayer-like invocation of divine intercession ('Gott wird mir den Kämpen schicken, ich bin schuldlos...'), and an anxiously empathetic chorus set to slow but restless harmonies, out of which a triumphant D-major, stretta-like episode (with requisite harmonic intensifications) suddenly emerges when Ivanhoe at last appears. Wagner, however, avoids Marschner's diffuseness, reducing these elements to a ritualistic simplicity. A comparison of the music of Lohengrin's arrival with the square-cut chorus that greets Ivanhoe tellingly encapsulates the relation of Wagner's 'Romantic operas' to their generic forbears, and explains something of Wagner's impatience with the German operatic tradition from which he emerged.

22

Above: Lohengrin *at the Royal Opera House in 1935: Lotte Lehmann, Alex Hirzel and*
Alexander Kipnis (Royal Opera House Archives)
Below: Lohengrin *in Munich, 1929 (Bayerische Staatsoper)*

II
The dramaturgy of musical 'colour'

The really productive element in Wagner is seen at the moments
when the subjective abdicates sovereignty and passively abandons
itself to the archaic, the instinctual — the element which, precisely
because it has been emancipated, renounces its now unattainable
claim to give meaningful shape to the passage of time. This element,
with its two dimensions of harmony and colour, is sonority. Through
sonority, time seems transfixed in space, and while as harmony it
'fills' space, the notion of colour, for which musical theory has no
better name, is directly borrowed from the realm of visual space. At
the same time, it is mere sonority which actually represents that
unarticulated natural state into which Wagner dissolves.

Theodor Adorno *In Search of Wagner*

Whatever it is, precisely, that Adorno is here imputing to Wagner, the
passage can be aptly applied to his Lohengrin, who appears from and
returns to — 'regresses' or 'dissolves' into — a state of pure sonority: an A
major chord sustained by widely-spaced violins and solo-violin harmonics.
(One wonders what the demanding opening bars of the Prelude must have
sounded like in 1850, when the Weimar court orchestra was augmented for
the occasion, not to speak of the numerous productions by ambitious
provincial German theatres over the next decades.) The exploitation of
orchestral colour for purposes of dramatic and scenic characterisation has
been singled out as a feature of the score since its première. Adorno cites
Richard Strauss's observation that each of Wagner's operas develops a
characteristic sonority or distinctive orchestral palette, and adds: 'for all his
expansion of the apparatus of instrumentation, Wagner's orchestra is
essentially intimate: ... the voices of the instruments address him, magical
and familiar, as colours are to children. And in fact the authentic conception
of Wagner's orchestral art [coincides] with his turning towards the intimate
in *Lohengrin*.' It is also with *Lohengrin*, Adorno claims, that instrumentation
is 'emancipated' from a subordinate position and assumes an integral role
in the definition of the musical substance or structure. The association of
Elsa with the sound of a muted woodwind choir, for instance, is explained
by Adorno as a means of translating the sound of the organ (in itself too
weak and commonplace for sustained deployment in opera) into a more
penetrating orchestral equivalent, an organ-like timbre that could
disseminate the connotations of a marriage ceremony through the score.[5]
Adorno interprets this role of musical 'colour' in Wagner's opera as an
element of both composition and of drama and as a progressive feature that
sets it apart from previous music, even from Berlioz (through here he surely
exaggerates).

Liszt was the first to remark on the conscious, 'structural' applications
of orchestral colour in *Lohengrin* in the brochure he published a year after

5 'The medieval-Romantic spirit of "minster" and "*Kemenate*" [the ladies quarters] inspires an
allusion to the timbre of the organ — to evoke the ideal image of an all-embracing cosmos
confirmed by God — and the woodwinds serve to create this archaic picture.' The oboe in place
of Elsa's silences in her first scene is glossed by Werner Breig with a quotation from Berlioz's
treatise on orchestration: according to Berlioz, the oboe is especially suited to the expression of
'naive grace, pure innocence, silent joy, and the sorrows of a sensitive nature' (Breig, 'The Musical
Works', *Wagner Handbook, ibid.*).

the première (*'Lohengrin' et 'Tannhäuser' de Richard Wagner*, Paris and Leipzig, 1851). 'Instead of combining or dividing [the various instrumental families] according to conventional or arbitrary practice, [Wagner] prefers to treat them as distinct bodies, carefully matching their timbral character to that of the dramatic situations or characters. This manner of orchestration is among the most striking features of his manner of composition, and the one which first commands our attention.' Liszt goes on to note the association of woodwind with the role of Elsa, the use of divided strings in a high register to evoke the realm of the Grail, and the consistent use of brass and stage trumpets to accompany the appearances of the King. Such consistent instrumental associations or attributes take on a kind of leimotivic aspect, as Liszt intimates.

Charles Baudelaire, who had been meditating on synaesthetic 'correspondences' or 'reciprocal analogies' between colours, scents and sounds when he encountered the Prelude under Wagner's baton in Paris in 1860, was impressed by the manner in which Wagner's music evoked the experience of solitary reverie and images of an 'immense horizon' and a 'vast, diffuse luminosity'. In 'Richard Wagner et Tannhäuser à Paris', an essay he published in the *Revue européenne* in 1861, Baudelaire drew attention to the congruence between his 'visual' experience of the Prelude and the descriptions provided by Wagner and Liszt, which he had not known at the time of the concerts. 'I experienced the sensation of ever-increasing clarity, of an intensity of light growing with such rapidity that no terms furnished by the dictionary could suffice to express this continuously renewed intensification of warmth and whiteness.' Baudelaire's description suggests that it is this spectrum of lightness and darkness, as much as the suggestion of 'colour' (properly speaking), that especially characterises the *Lohengrin* score. The drama itself deals in polarities of 'black and white' in a way that is hardly typical of his other operas (characterising here, of course, the antimonies of profane and sacred, pagan and Christian). Lohengrin is the archetypal 'white knight' and Elsa his virginal 'fair lady'. 'I did not come from night and sadness: from light and joy I journeyed here!' ('Denn nicht komm' ich aus Nacht und Leiden, aus Glanz und Wonne kam ich her!'), Lohengrin assures Elsa in their last, fateful dialogue in Act Three, to a firm cadence in his 'native' key of A major.[6] Ortrud is a practitioner of black arts, and once ensnared by her, Friedrich von Telramund becomes cast, *de facto*, as Lohengrin's antipode, the black knight. The central scene concerning Ortrud and Friedrich (Act Two, scene 1), takes place entirely at night, and within the controlling orbit of F sharp minor, relative minor to Lohengrin's A major, or its tonal opposite.

Even though Baudelaire prided himself on having 'discovered' the colours and images of the score, Wagner had given the cue for such synaesthetic responses in his programme-note to the Prelude, where he describes the materialization of a Grail-bearing angelic host 'out of the brightest blue heavenly ether' gradually coming nearer and nearer, until the Grail itself is revealed (an anticipation of *Parsifal*) at the climax. Wagner

6 In *A Communication to my Friends* Wagner draws a parallel between the Lohengrin story and the myth of Zeus and Semele, in which Semele is annihilated by the 'blinding light' that emanates from the god when revealed in his true form. While *Tannhäuser* revolves around a similar axis of sacred and profane forces, the colour spectrum differs from that in *Lohengrin*. The erotic underworld of Venus is characterized by 'rosy mists', in Wagner's own words, while the world of the knights and *Minnesänger* is a world of 'healthy, natural beauties — of green forests, blue skies and, perhaps, the simple, bright primary colours of medieval courtly ceremony.

describes this from the perspective of the experiencing subject, to whom he attributes such characteristically Wagnerian states as 'the swelling of all the overpowering seeds of love', a feeling of 'wondrous increase', a 'mighty yearning', and a drive towards the yielding or 'surrender' and finally the 'dissolution' of the self altogether. He even adds a further dimension to the synaesthetic experience of the Prelude when he speaks of the 'delightful scents' that waft from the golden nimbus surrounding this vision. The whole is described as an immediate, overwhelming *sensory* experience, in which any conceptual imagery (angels, Grail) is secondary. The climax evokes images of the 'sunbeams of sublimest love', the 'glow of divine fire' (whose intensity brings about the 'loss of sense altogether' as the subject falls prostrate), which quickly subside to reveal once again the ethereal blue while the angelic host retreats. (The trope of a religious ecstasy imbued with strong erotic overtones in the tradition of St Theresa can also be recognized in Isolde's 'transfiguration' or 'Liebestod'.) Thus while the musical motifs and 'sound-imagery' of the Prelude are all logically associated with the figure of Lohengrin and his mission, the Prelude may represent *Elsa*'s visionary intuition of her champion (which she later describes), since Wagner's account of the Prelude so strongly emphasizes the role of the passive 'viewer' or subject and would appear to ascribe a distinctly feminine identity to that subject, in the tradition of divinely-inspired ecstasies.

Since at least the time of Guido Adler's lectures on Wagner at the University of Vienna (1904), Wagner's use of certain tonalities more or less systematically in conjunction with instrumental timbres has been taken to be a significant stage in the development of his mature 'leitmotif' techniques. Wagner insisted, in an often-cited letter to his friend Uhlig (May 31, 1852), that the 'character' of keys was inseparable from their empirical effect on instrumental timbres. The divided strings of the opening Grail-music recur always in the key of A, as mentioned — the key that is associated with Lohengrin as a miraculous emissary. In Act One Wagner contrasts the 'brightness' of that key — whether in the high strings or trumpets or full orchestra, when the vision of Lohengrin becomes incarnate — with the 'softer', dreamy character of Elsa's flat keys (especially A flat) and her characteristic woodwinds. Ortrud's music in Act Two and in the final scene revolves around F sharp minor, the opposite pole of Lohengrin's A major.

Wagner also establishes the effect of his 'associative' keys by means of striking tonal juxtapositions. Elsa's visionary motif [6] moves from E flat or A flat out to A or D (as if intuiting the tonal domain of her champion) and back again. A flat remains the 'principal key' (as Wagner would probably have put it) throughout the scene of her interrogation by King Henry, yielding immediately to A major at the moment Lohengrin is sighted, by means of the same modulations embedded within her own motif. A more pointed juxtaposition occurs in the next scene, when Lohengrin announces the 'forbidden question'. At first he speaks to her sweetly and solicitously in her own key of A flat for a moment ('Wenn ich im Kampfe für dich siege, willst du, dass ich dein Gatte sei?' 'If I'm victorious in the contest, will you agree to marry me?'), and she answers in a state of dreamy contentment. In the same state (and key) she responds distractedly to Lohengrin's injunction ('Nie sollst du mich befragen, noch Wissens Sorge tragen' 'My history is hidden, these questions are forbidden') upon which Lohengrin repeats his command sternly, a half-tone higher in A minor. She responds more emphatically in A major, the key of the chorus

26

hymn to Lohengrin, based on motivic ideas associated with the Grail (see [11]). A still more radical juxtaposition of key and timbre marks the juncture of the first and second scenes of Act Two. Here the F sharp minor principal key of the dialogue between the outcasts, Ortrud and Friedrich — prominently coloured by the timbre of the bass-clarinet with low strings — yields to B flat major (by means of a compact eight-bar modulation), high woodwinds, and an anticipation of the theme of Elsa's procession to the Minster, as she leans out of her balcony to take the night air (see example 2).

Example 2
Mäßig langsam

The consistent association between King Henry (and retinue) and the C major sonority of stage trumpets may be attributed to conventional practice and the practical limitations of natural trumpets. But Wagner's use of this stock association of key and timbre is enhanced by reinterpreting the tones of the C major triad within an ever-changing variety of tonal contexts (usually as part of a dominant or diminished seventh chord in some other key). In this he anticipates the similar treatments of the 'sword' motif — another C major trumpet flourish — throughout the *Ring*.

Cheryl Studer as Elsa and Paul Frey as Lohengrin at Covent Garden, 1988 (photo: Clive Barda)

III
Reminiscence motifs and Leitmotif

Lohengrin is most distinctively transitional with respect to two defining features of the mature Wagnerian music drama: the continuity of melodic-musical discourse at the level of the scene and the development of the 'leitmotif' idea. It is, of course, the leitmotif that is largely responsible for the possibility of 'infinite melody' and the continuity of dramatic musical discourse deriving from it. *Lohengrin*'s anticipation of the leitmotif technique of the music dramas is one more indication of the (sometimes uneasy) equilibrium between convention and experiment that characterises the score. The origins of the technique of motivic reminiscence in German Romantic opera and the *grand opéra* of Meyerbeer are well-documented: the operas of Weber, and particularly his *Euryanthe*, are often cited as the most significant precursors of Wagner's leimotif technique but Liszt, in his 1851 brochure, pointed to Meyerbeer's *Huguenots* as a precedent, with its use of the Lutheran chorale, 'A Mighty Fortress is Our God'; Raimbaut's ballad-tune ('Jadis regnait en Normandie') is also used in much the same way in *Robert le diable*. The simpler practice of citing a complete theme or some larger unit (such as a stanza from a strophic song) was a standard operatic device by the 1840s. One effective example of reminiscence motif in *Lohengrin* is the recollection of the complete eight-bar phrase from the Lohengrin-Elsa 'duet' in Act Three, scene 2 ('Fühl' ich zu dir so süss mein Herz entbrennen' 'Here in my heart a flame is brightly burning' [25]) softly in the clarinet at the end of the scene; it emerges wistfully from the stunned near-silence that follows the catastrophe of the 'forbidden question' and the ambush of Lohengrin by the conspirators.

By the time he had completed *Lohengrin*, however, Wagner was already aware of the potential of a more developed network of motivic reminiscences and allusions. In *A Communication to my Friends* (1852) he reflected on this still evolving conception of motifs, acknowledging precedents but at the same time emphasising a distinction between simple reminiscence and a dramatically motivated transformation of thematic material (Umbildung des thematischen Stoffes) such as he claimed to have initiated in his most recent score:

> Beyond his, my procedure began to assume a more distinctive artistic form — particularly in *Lohengrin* by means of a continuous transformation of the thematic material in accordance with the character of the situation. This resulted in a musically more varied application of the procedure than had been the case, for instance, in my *Flying Dutchman*, where the recurrence of themes often retained the character of an absolute reminiscence (in which practice other composers had preceded me).

Not all of the motivic recurrences in *Lohengrin* involve extensive development but Wagner does demonstrate an ever-increasing ingenuity in adapting motifs to dramatic situations. Lohengrin's motif [8], for instance, can be reduced from its original eight-bar form (not counting its sequential consequent) to four or even two bars and still retain its identity. But rather than subject his head-motif to developmental processes, Wagner tends simply to apply the kinds of colouristic and tonal variation discussed above. In Elsa's dream-narration (Act One, scene 2), for instance, the motif is 'anticipated' (in the terms of *Opera and Drama*) in a quiet, 'distant' scoring for high winds against a *pianissimo* accompaniment of harp and tremolo strings, in A-flat. When Lohengrin is sighted in the distance, the motif issues softly from three trumpets (still again in *pianissimo* string tremolo), now in A major. When he stands fully revealed before the people, or when he later wields his sword over Friedrich in triumph, the motif sounds in the full orchestra, and again in A. The full melody is heard one last time, *tutti* and in A major, as Lohengrin embarks for his homeward journey, but the head-motif echoes mournfully in the woodwind, in the minor mode and *piano*, as his figure is glimpsed receding into the distance. Similarly, the motif, of the 'forbidden question' [12] has its dramaturgical roots in a repertoire of operatic curses, incantatory formulas and solemn oaths — which are naturally disposed to treatment as reminiscence motifs. (By the same token, it anticipates the role of such motifs as Alberich's 'renunciation of love' and his curse on the Ring in *Das Rheingold*.) Like Lohengrin's motif, that of the 'forbidden question' originates as a complete eight-bar phrase, whose distinctive opening bars are sufficient to announce its identity and purpose. These bars may ring out in the manner of an ominous curse, as at the end of Act Two (trumpets and trombones, F minor), or they may be embedded as a discreet accompanimental fragment, suggesting a suppressed subconscious warning, as happens several times during the bridal-chamber scene (Act Three, scene 2) before resounding curse-like again at its climax.

It is the figure of Ortrud, with her malign cunning and accomplished sorcery, who inspires the most extensive, varied and 'advanced' implementation of motivic reminiscence, weaving her motivic identity about herself and her victims like an evil spell. Consequently, it is the one scene in which Ortrud plays the leading role — the first scene of Act Two — where Wagner most closely approaches the mature leitmotivic technique, the continuously evolving forms and 'infinite melody', of the later music dramas. Ortrud's motivic material resembles the leitmotivic substance of the *Ring* (the 'Ring' motif itself, for example) in its fragmentary, melodically and harmonically open-ended contours, unlike the tonally and periodically stable outlines of most other thematic elements in *Lohengrin*. The three modular components of this motivic 'complex' (see example 3a-c) are rooted in two diminished-seventh chords and hence, like the harmonically equivocal 'Ring' motif, are not only suitably sinister in effect, but can be easily integrated into all sorts of musical contexts.

This versatility is exploited throughout the opera. In this scene even the two independent musical numbers — Friedrich's old-fashioned 'rage' aria and the conspiratorial duet — are subtly informed by the serpentine contours of Ortrud's motifs. Another anticipatory touch is the 'associational magic' or motivic allusiveness (Bezeihungszauber) that Thomas Mann admires in the leimotif technique of the later works, which is produced here by the intervallic and rhythmic proximity of Ortrud's initial motif (example 3a) to the opening of the 'forbidden question' motif. This ambiguity is illustrated in the instrumental prologue where Wagner joins the head-motif of Ortrud's complex to the second phrase of the 'forbidden question' (example 4). The motif-complex associated with Ortrud appropriately contributes to the seamless melodic discourse that conveys those unspoken or suppressed subconscious motivations for which Wagnerian music drama is so famous.

In thoroughly contrasting ways, Ortrud's motivic complex and the music of Lohengrin's Grail-realm have one quality in common: a tendency to 'hover', seemingly ungrounded, in musical space. The Grail music appears to hover shimmering and diaphanous in empyrean diatonic heights and brilliant sunlight: Ortrud's motifs hover in dark, diminished depths of night. (Their hovering is determined in some degree by a rhythmic flaccidity that besets the *Lohengrin* score — a condition of which Wagner was aware, and on which he ruminated briefly in following years. Nietzsche considered such 'hovering' to be a characteristic of Wagner's 'endless melody'.) Similarly, *Lohengrin* (as a whole) 'hovers' — between the traditions of a recent operatic past and the innovations of a Wagnerian 'artwork of the future'. Even the stage setting is symptomatic of the condition. On the one hand it is grounded in a precise historical milieu in the manner of *grand opéra* (the fractious duchy of Brabant in the early tenth century), which affords all the panoply of ceremony as well as a hierarchy of political power-relations to activate the plot. On the other hand, the figure of Lohengrin establishes a link to another domain, that of Christian myth and of mythic archetypes, that is crucial to Wagner's theory of the perfected, 'purely-human' dramatic art-work. Whether the possible friction between the domains of history and myth, or between those of *grand opéra* (with its foundation in effective numbers and tableaux) and music drama (with its ideal of 'naturalistic' dramatic continuity) is aesthetically productive, or whether it is an aesthetic liability, is not a question open to simple resolution. It is just these historical and aesthetic tensions behind Wagner's last 'opera', nonetheless, that contribute to its indeterminate character of 'no longer' but 'not yet' (as the Germans are fond of saying). And this indeterminate character by no means detracted from the work's contemporary appeal and influence. On the contrary, *Lohengrin* remained the most often performed of Wagner's works until the end of the nineteenth century. One source of this appeal lay in the very fact that it offered audiences a cautious taste of the modern music drama, while preserving a recognizable foundation in comfortably familiar operatic traditions.

Example 3
Mäßig langsam

Example 4
Mäßig langsam

Maria Nezádal, the Czech soprano, as Elsa in Munich, 1927 (Bayersische Staatsoper)

History, Women's History, and Beyond History in 'Lohengrin'

Janet L. Nelson

Lohengrin, Elsa and Wagner

In *A Communication to my Friends*, Wagner explained that the story of Lohengrin embodied a universal myth about the union of the human with the sublime. Two worlds were symbolically linked by a waterway: the wild, animal world of nature and the controlled 'higher' world of supernature. The river-bank — scene of so much of the action in Wagner's *Lohengrin* — was the margin between them. The swan-knight moved between the two worlds. He embodied the divine, entering the human world in supernatural fashion, a stranger, of superhuman strength and virtue. But the swan-knight also embodied the human, indeed 'the most quintessential essence of human nature', for he journeyed of his own volition, drawn by 'the necessity of love, the longing for utmost physical reality.' Wagner had reacted with some 'suspicion and repugnance' to the anonymous thirteenth-century epic *Lohengrin*, shrouded as he thought in the religious paraphernalia of Catholicism. By contrast Konrad von Würzburg's *The Swan Knight*, which Wagner took to be the 'simpler' and 'deeper' form of the Lohengrin story, seemed an 'eternal poem', 'the genuine poem of the folk', expressive of 'pure humanity'.

'Genuine'; 'original'; 'pure': in Wagner's vocabulary, the adjectives used to describe the myth of Lohengrin also defined the quintessential woman. Elsa's centrality to the poem had a political as well as personal dimension. 'Elsa, the woman . . . this most necessary embodiment of the purest physical spontaneity, made a total revolutionary of me. She was the spirit of the people by whom I, too, as man and artist, longed to be redeemed.' Wagner had found an escape from the dead-end of elite art and assuaged his anxiety over audiences' responses to his work. From the medieval past, through the character of Elsa, he retrieved a sense of the people (the *Volk*) as a potentially universal audience. In the character of Ortrud, Wagner invented a scarcely less universal antitype for Elsa. Between them, the two women, emblems of pure and impure power, represented the totality of an imagined past. Hence, in his own *Lohengrin*, Wagner claimed to have 'provided a complete picture of the Middle Ages'.

Wagner was an artist, not a professional historian: he was less interested in medieval history as such than in medieval literary works and folk-tales. For him, as for so many writers of the late eighteenth and nineteenth centuries, the medieval world provided a plausible setting for the portrayal of the human condition. But what he conceived as timeless was in fact time-bound — bound, that is, to Wagner's own time. To quote a recent critic, Volker Mertens: 'Wagner believed that he himself was the first person to have extracted the essential mythical meaning of [the] medieval narratives and to have portrayed that meaning onstage, whereas what he actually staged . . . were the problems of his own age, even of his own life.' Nevertheless, in placing two powerful women centre-stage, in making the conflict between Elsa and Ortrud the driving-force of his drama, and their confrontation its highpoint, Wagner reproduced medieval realities more faithfully than he knew. In the later twentieth century, the study of women's history has revealed the play of gender through medieval politics and religion, just as late-twentieth-century political concerns have lent a new topicality to the European setting of *Lohengrin*.

Lotharingia and Europe

Wagner's 'Middle Ages' formed an undifferentiated thousand-year period between antiquity and modern times, and covered a geographical space vaguely understood as coterminous with western Europe. Elements of the Lohengrin myth, however, reflect specifically the impact of the Carolingian period, that is, the reigns of Charlemagne, ruler of the Franks (768-814) and his ninth- and tenth-century successors. The name 'Lohengrin' evokes what the French call Lorraine, the Germans Lothringen, nowadays a relatively small region in eastern France. The original Lotharingia was a much larger kingdom that briefly existed in the ninth century, taking its name from Lothar, Charlemagne's eldest grandson. It included the heart of Charlemagne's empire between the rivers Scheldt and Rhine, lands in which lay the great Carolingian palaces of Nijmegen and Aachen. The Carolingian heartlands, in fact, consisted of what is now the core-area of the EEC, between, say, Brussels, Maastricht and Strasbourg, just as the Carolingian Empire covered approximately the area of the original six community states: France, Germany, the Benelux countries, and Italy.

None of this is coincidental. After the reign of Charlemagne's sole surviving son Louis the Pious (814-40), and a three-year war of succession, the Carolingian Empire was split in 843 between Lothar and his younger brothers, Louis of 'Germany', and Charles of 'France'. In economic terms,

Alexander Kipnis as King Henry at Covent Garden in 1935 (Royal Opera House Archives)

Lotharingia could well have seemed more viable than 'France' or 'Germany'. In fact it was a kingdom without a future. Lothar's son and namesake failed to produce a legitimate heir; and on his death in 869, his two uncles split Lotharingia between them. In the century that followed, France and Germany took shape, but the division-line between them proved unstable. For both eastern and western kingdoms, Lotharingia remained a marginal zone, resistant to control. For a millennium, a great fault-line has run through the heart of western Europe, as France and Germany have warred, recurrently, over the kingdom that might have been. Since the Second World War, the impetus for reconciliation has come from the Rhineland, from Alsace and Lorraine, from the Benelux countries — in short, from the ancient lands of Lotharingia.

Yet the Carolingian Empire also bequeathed a common inheritance to its successor-states in east and west. The unity of Latin Europe was rooted in shared experience of Frankish political dominance, of Christian kingship supported by a warrior elite, of power legitimised by warfare against the heathen. In the eighth century, Charlemagne had imposed Christianity on pagan Frisians and Saxons. Under his successors in the ninth and tenth centuries, Scandinavians, Slavs and Hungarians more or less willingly accepted Christianity. Europe's unity was also a unity of shared myths: Charlemagne's raid into Muslim Spain in 778 had been recast, by the eleventh century, as a first attempt at Reconquest. The men who went on the First Crusade called themselves *Franci*, and saw themselves as the heirs of Charlemagne's Franks. In 1099, they captured Jerusalem. Their leader, Godfrey (Gottfried), was descended from the highest nobility of Lotharingia.

Rodney Godshall as King Henry and Michael Vier as the Herald in John Dew's production, designed by Heinz Balthes, in Bielefeld, 1991 (photo: F. Stockmeier/Opera Magazine)

Women in medieval culture

The making of Christendom was the work of churchmen and of warriors; but it was also the work of women. In pagan societies, in eighth-century Frisia or Saxony for instance, women operated through marriage and the family, educating their offspring, producing and reproducing households. Women were thus key transmitters of heathen religion. Christianity's official attitude to women, on the other hand, had always been profoundly ambivalent. Since the Early Church, ecclesiastical stereotypes of women had been polarised between the temptress and the redemptress, the whore and the virgin. Women's sexuality was perceived as at once necessary to Christendom's perpetuation, yet darkly dangerous. The practice of pagan magic was denounced and penalised specifically as a woman's offence. Christianisation required, not the abandonment of gendered stereotypes, but their re-evaluation: women were to become the Church's agents. Christian missionaries targeted women, acknowledging their familial power, re-casting them as the keepers of Christian family-consciousness and educators of Christian children. In the ninth century, churchmen, intent on defusing the mysteries of women's sexual conduct, introduced special forms of judicial ordeal to deal with women accused of sexual offences. Offered access to alternative powers of healing and fertility, women (especially mothers) eagerly took up the cults of the saints. Monasteries thrived on the benefactions of female donors. Saint-queens specialised in Christian nurturing. The motif of the Christian wife converting her pagan husband proliferated in ecclesiastical histories. Priestly confessors encouraged wives to concern themselves with their husbands' spiritual welfare 'even in the marriage bed'. Women — low-born as well as high-born, in house or hovel as well as hall — had become part of Christian mythology. Here, gender overrode status or class: women's power was homogenous at whatever social level, and it was diffused through whole populations. Wagner saw this as a power 'of the people', hence with a potentially universal force. For all his 1840s idealism (amply shared by Karl Marx — *The Communist Manifesto* and *Lohengrin* are almost exactly contemporary), he had a valid historical point.

One example touches the Lohengrin story directly. Wagner's opera opens with the arrival of Emperor Henry the Fowler. The historical Henry was the first non-Carolingian ruler of the German *Reich* (919-36). He took as wife Matilda, descendant of the pagan leader Widukind who had led the Saxon resistance to Charlemagne. As queen, and later as dowager in the reign of her son Otto the Great (936-73), Matilda wielded political influence ('she used to sit while everyone else stood'). At the same time, she took special responsibility for the Christian commemoration of the dead of her husband's family, and prayers for the success of its living members in war against the pagan Hungarians. Venerated as a saint soon after her own death, Matilda wielded supernatural powers believed to secure the realm's fertility. In 996, her great-grandson Otto offered his sister to the church as a nun, to appease divine wrath during a terrible famine and yet another pagan onslaught.

In the eleventh and twelfth centuries, and not least in the old lands of Lotharingia, new currents of reforming Christian piety flowed through women. Wives urged their husbands to join the Crusade, and mothers brought up their sons in what swiftly became familial traditions of crusading. This was the second crucially formative period for medieval western Christendom. It was in the twelfth century that the folk-tales underpinning the plot of *Lohengrin* were first recorded in writing, in courtly poems and romances, as part of elite European culture. Wagner's poem was woven out of later medieval versions of those texts. But twelfth-century change was not just about writing down hitherto oral traditions. This was a change of substance as well as form. Whereas the epics of the earlier Middle Ages were about lordship and kinship and the comradeship of warriors, the central themes in twelfth-century literature came to be love and marriage. Literature reflected life. The twelfth century saw the discovery of the individual. The Church professionalised itself: recruitment of its personnel through individual choice, and individual merit, was the means by which the institution could be freed from the shackles of family-interest. Monasteries were now to be filled with men and women who had experienced conversion as adults, and, after a century of criticism, the offering of children by parents was finally forbidden by the Fourth Lateran Council in 1215. An individual could choose from a variety of new religious orders, or s/he might choose the solitary hermit's life. Women as well as men opted in some cases for unofficial, even unorthodox, religion: popular heresy became a problem for the Church — and the word 'heresy' means choice. There was personal choice in lay life too: between military and mercantile careers, or colonising enterprise. This was a world of self-made men. The knight choosing his quest was as solitary as the hermit. But the knight also hoped to choose a bride.

The twelfth century was the age of the heiress. For the first time, aristocratic women were permitted to inherit not only lands but principalities and even kingdoms. A few women did wield such power in their own right; many more transmitted power to husbands and sons. Aspiring young men achieved greatness through marriage. Princes eagerly seized opportunities: in 1138, the young heir to the French throne vastly increased his power by marrying Eleanor, the heiress to Aquitaine. This change came about not through conflict but confluence of lay with ecclesiastical interests. The dynastic strategies of kings and nobles required the preservation of inheritances, hence primogeniture, and the discarding of younger sons. Political order, in which the Church had a strong stake, required the smooth transmission of high office. In the twelfth century, powerful laymen colluded in the Church's take-over of jurisdiction in marital cases: here, where dishonour and conflict were most likely to arise, the acceptance of ecclesiastical judgement, based on legal argument and bureaucratic procedure, enabled men to save face. Ordeals were now abandoned in practice, surviving only in song and story. Church lawyers applied the notion of individual commitment to marriage, insisting on the consent of both spouses as constitutive, and on life-long monogamy as the norm.

Lay men adapted their behaviour to the new rules. The descent of a family's power now hinged on the partnership of spouses, the solidarity of husband with wife. Medieval medical lore taught that the conception of a child was possible only when both partners enjoyed the sexual act. A loveless marriage, one in which the woman was unsatisfied, would produce no heir. Such beliefs created conditions in which aristocratic women, at least, might benefit from a new consideration for their personal wishes. Some acquired a measure of self-determination in their lives. Convinced that she would never bear him a son, Louis VII of France divorced Eleanor of Aquitaine: she chose to marry again, this time the heir to the English throne, the future Henry II, and so Louis lost control of a third of his kingdom. When twelfth-century poets expressed a heightened awareness of the power of love, they idealised, but also reflected, new social realities: no Golden Age for women, certainly, but an age when a few women of high status could command, through and within marriage, rather more attention than before.

The old myths and the new

Myths too reflected marriage's enhanced importance, and its attendant risks, from the viewpoint of both spouses. Melusine was the fairy-woman who came out of the water, or from the depths of the forest, and bestowed the goods of the earth on a mortal husband. He was forbidden to know her identity: violation of the prohibition led to the husband's loss of his fairy-wife. The swan-knight was heaven-sent, gaining earthly power through marriage to an earthly bride. She could not know his identity: violation of that prohibition led to the wife's loss of her mysterious husband. The audience for these stories consisted of women, as well as men, who set a premium on marriage as a partnership and were concerned for its survival over time.

The twelfth century was also the age of the prophet concerned with understanding, and predicting, religious time, and the end of time. From 1099 onwards, when Christian warriors won Jerusalem on the First Crusade, western Christians sensed themselves to be living in a new era — of hope, but also of anxiety. Christendom's identity was then expressed above all in the experience, and the mythology, of crusading, which offered a justification of earthly power derived from the sword. Chivalry involved a new kind of warfare, embracing religious goals and the service of a noble lady. The crusaders created a kingdom in Outremer, 'the land beyond the sea'. The Melusine legend was attached to two of the most successful of the 'new' noble families of France, the Angevins and the Lusignans; it explained their demonic power. Both families came to be associated with Outremer: first Fulk of Anjou, then Guy of Lusignan, married heiresses to the kingdom of Jerusalem, and so became kings themselves. When Jerusalem was recaptured by Muslim armies in 1187, the ideology of the Crusade shifted, becoming detached from a specific terrain and from merely human chronology. The Grail legend etherealised the crusading quest. The leader of the First Crusade, Godfrey, was said to have refused a crown, taking instead the title of protector of the Holy Sepulchre. The kingdom of Jerusalem moved beyond time. Myth recovered its own.

From Lotharingia, Charlemagne had gone out to war against Spanish Muslims, and Henry the Fowler to victory over pagan Hungarians. *Lohengrin's* setting is the Low Countries, where Charlemagne had made Nijmegen a major palace, on the frontier with recently-converted Frisia. In the French versions of the Lohengrin story, supernatural ancestry was supplied for Godfrey, future leader of the successful Crusade, as the grandson of the Swan-Knight. Godfrey's father was count of Boulogne but his mother Ida was the daughter of the Swan-Knight. Once again legitimate power passed through a woman, and history was combined with myth. While Elsa appears at the beginning and end of the opera as the sister of Gottfried, transmitter of power to her younger brother, the focus for

Lohengrin *in the 1971 Sadler's Wells production at the London Coliseum by Colin Graham,*
designed by Michael Knight and conducted by Charles Mackerras.
Above: Act One, with Clifford Grant as King Henry and Margaret Curphey as Elsa.
Below: Act Two, with Alberto Remedios as Lohengrin.
(photos: John Garner)

Wagner, as for the German poet of the *Swan-Knight*, is on the bride not as potential mother but as wife: the wife of Lohengrin.

In *Lohengrin's* opposed images of female power, Wagner reproduced the ambivalence of medieval Christian tradition. Ortrud presents the obverse side of that power: denizen of dark forests, prophetess, practitioner of magic arts, descendant of a people burdened by centuries of unhappiness, embodiment of ancestral paganism, bewitcher of the boy Gottfried. Elsa is the reverse: her purity vindicated by the ordeal, she represents the rightful order of the noble Christian line of Lotharingia, the apt transmitter of divinely-approved power when Lohengrin entrusts her with insignia (horn, sword, ring) to pass to her brother, and, most important of all, the embodiment of human love. Wagner's careful stage-directions make women themselves the sensitive indicators of this polarity: they shrink from Ortrud, cluster around Elsa. Women, for Wagner as for medieval churchmen, could not be neutral: charged with symbolic meaning, they represented the forces of good and evil at work in, and beyond, history.

Gabriele Schnaut as Ortrud with Paul Frey as Lohengrin at Covent Garden, 1988 (photo: Clive Barda)

Lohengrin in Brabant

Jacob and Wilhelm Grimm

The Duke of Brabant and Limburg died without leaving any other heirs apart from a young daughter, Els or Elsam, whom he commended on his deathbed to one of his vassals, Frederick of Telramund. Frederick, otherwise a doughty hero, who had slain a dragon at Stockholm in Sweden, grew overbearing and sued for the young duchess's hand and lands under the false pretext that she had promised to marry him. Since she steadfastly refused him, Frederick complained to the emperor, Henry the Fowler; and it was adjudged that she must defend herself in an ordeal by calling on the services of a hero. When no such hero could be found, the duchess prayed ardently to God for deliverance. Far away at Montsalvat in the kingdom of the Grail the bell began to peal as a sign that someone needed help urgently; forthwith the Grail resolved to send out Lohengrin, Parzival's son. The latter was just on the point of placing his foot in his stirrup when a swan came gliding over the water, drawing a boat behind it. Scarcely had Lohengrin glimpsed it when he cried out: 'Return the horse to the manger; I shall go with this bird, wherever it takes me.' Trusting in God, he took no food with him in the boat; after they had travelled for five days over the sea, the swan plunged its beak beneath the waves, caught a fish, ate half of it and gave the other half to the prince to eat.

Meanwhile Elsam had summoned her princes and vassals to a diet at Antwerp. On the very day the assembly met, a swan was seen swimming up the Scheldt, drawing a little boat in which Lohengrin slept, stretched out on his shield. The swan soon swam ashore, and the prince was joyfully welcomed; scarcely had his helmet, shield and sword been lifted out of the boat when the swan swam off the way it had come. Lohengrin heard the injustice the duchess had suffered and gladly agreed to be her champion. Elsam thereupon sent for all her kinsmen and subjects, who arrived in large numbers, ready to help; even King Gotthart, her maternal grandsire, came from England, summoned hither by Gundemar, the abbot of Clarbrunn. The procession set out, with the rest of the company joining it at Saarbrück, from where they made their way to Mainz. Emperor Henry, who was staying at Frankfurt, came to meet them in Mainz, and it was here the lists were set up where Lohengrin and Frederick were to fight. The Grail's hero triumphed; Frederick confessed to having falsely accused the duchess and was sentenced to death by beheading. Elsam was now bestowed upon Lohengrin, and they loved one another for many a year; but he secretly made her promise not to ask any questions about his origins; otherwise he would straightway have to leave her.

For a time the couple lived together in a state of unalloyed happiness, and Lohengrin ruled the country wisely and powerfully; he also rendered the emperor sterling service on his campaigns against the Huns and heathens. But it came about that he one day unhorsed the Duke of Cleves in a joust and broke the latter's arm; spitefully the Duchess of Cleves then noised it abroad among the womenfolk: 'A brave hero Lohengrin may very well be, and he seems to share the Christian faith; a pity his fame is so slight in terms of his nobility; for no one know whence he came to this land.' These words cut the Duchess of Brabant to the quick, and she blushed and

41

blanched. That night in bed, when her husband held her in his arms, she began to weep; he said: 'My love, what ails thee?' She answered: 'It is the Duchess of Cleves who has made me sigh so deeply,' but Lohengrin said nothing and asked no more questions. The second night she started to weep once again; and again he noticed and staunched her tears. Only on the third night could Elsam no longer restrain herself and said: 'My lord, do not be angry with me! I fain would know your place of birth; for my heart tells me you do not lack nobility.' When day broke, Lohengrin explained in public whence he had come; Parzival was his father and God had sent him here from the Grail. Thereupon he sent for both the children that the duchess had borne him, kissed them and bade them safeguard the horn and sword that he was leaving behind with them; to the duchess he gave the ring which his mother had once bequeathed to him. Then his friend, the swan, came swimming swiftly towards them, with the little boat behind it; the prince stepped into it and was carried away upstream in the service of the Grail. Elsam sank to the ground in a faint, so that her teeth had to be forced apart with a wedge and water poured down her throat. The emperor and empire took charge of the orphans; the children's names were Johann and Lohengrin. But the widow wept and throughout her remaining life bewailed her beloved husband, who nevermore returned.

This is the Grimms' summary of the Middle High German Lohengrin *of c1280, translated by Stewart Spencer.*

Peter Seiffert as Lohengrin and Lucia Popp as Elsa in Munich, 1989 (photo: Sabine Toepffer)

Thematic Guide

Many of the themes from this opera have been identified in the articles by numbers in square brackets, which refer to the themes set out on these pages. The themes are also identified by the numbers in square brackets at the corresponding points in the libretto, so that the words can be related to the musical themes.

[8]
Etwas belebt

[9]
Langsam

[10]
Langsam

LOHENGRIN I thank you, be - lov - ed friend! O - ver the wa - ter glide a - way.
Nun sei be - dankt, mein lie - berSchwan! Zieh' durch die wei - te Flut zu - rück.

[11]
Langsam

CHORUS What sense of won - der o - ver - comes us!
Wie faßt uns se - lig sü - ßes Grau - en!

[12]
sehr langsam *p*

LOHENGRIN My his - tor - y is hid - den,
Nie sollst du mich be - fra - gen,

[13]
feierlich

KING My Lord and God I pray to you may you be pre - sent at this fight,
Mein Herr und Gott, nun ruf' ich dich, daß du dem Kampf zu - ge - gen sei'st!

[14]
Sehr lebhaft

ELSA *ff* [O] could I find the words to ce - le - brate and raise
[O] fänd' ich Ju - bel - wei - sen, dein - nem Ruh - me gleich,

44

[15]
Mäßig langsam

p

[16]
Mäßig langsam

pp   *ff*   *dim.*   *pp*

ORTRUD/   My bit - ter heart cries out for ven - geance it will de - stroy the foe it hates;
FRIEDRICH   Der Ra - che Werk sei nun be schwo - ren aus mei - nes Bu -sens wil - der Nacht!

[17]
Langsam und feierlich

Clarinet
p

[18]
f

CHORUS 1   The trum - pet sum - mons us at dawn,
In Früh'n ver -samm - elt uns der Ruf;

[19]
ff

CHORUS   We'll bold - ly join the fray! On us his light has shone!__
Wer mu - thig mit ihm ficht, dem lacht des Ruh - mes Bahn!__

[20]
Langsam und feierlich

p

[21]
Sehr lebhaft

tr

ff
3

45

[22]

Sehr lebhaft

ff

[23]

Sehr lebhaft

p   *mf*   *dim.* *p*

[24]

Mäßig bewegt

p

CHORUS Hus - band and wife,   en - ter with - in,
          Treu - lich ge - führt   zie - het da - hin,

[25]

Noch etwas langsamer

pp

ELSA   Here in my heart a flame is bright - ly burn - ing
         Fühl ich zu dir so süß mein Herz ent -bren - nen,

[26]

Ruhig bewegs

pp

LOH.   Come, won't you share the night's mys -   ter -   ious per - fumes?
     Ath - mest du nicht mit mir die   sü -   ßen Düf - te?

Lohengrin

Romantic Opera in three acts

by Richard Wagner

English Translation by Amanda Holden

The first performance of *Lohengrin* was given in the Court Theatre at Weimar on August 28, 1850. The first performance in the United States was in New York on April 3, 1871. The first performance in Britain was on May 8, 1875, at Covent Garden (in Italian).

This German text follows the full score published by Breitkopf and Härtel in 1887. The translation was commissioned by English National Opera for a new production at the London Coliseum by Tim Albery, conducted by Mark Elder, on November 20, 1993.

The lay-out follows Wagner's setting of the text in the *Complete Works* and is indented according to the length of the lines — ten, eight or six syllables. It was prepared by Stewart Spencer, who also translated the stage directions.

The numbers in square brackets refer to the musical themes in the Thematic Guide.

THE CHARACTERS

Heinrich der Vogler/Henry the Fowler *the German King*	*bass*
Lohengrin	*tenor*
Elsa von Brabant/Elsa of Brabant	*soprano*
Friedrich von Telramund/Frederick of Telramund *a Count of Brabant*	*baritone*
Ortrud *his wife*	*soprano*
The King's Herald	*bass*
Four Nobles of Brabant	*tenors and basses*
Four Noble Pages	*sopranos and altos*

Saxon and Thuringian counts and nobles, Brabantine counts and nobles, Ladies in Waiting, Pages, Men, Women and Servants

The action takes place in Antwerp in the first half of the tenth century.

Wagner's sketch for the first act in the 1850 Weimar production

Act One

Scene One. *The curtain rises. A meadow on the banks of the Scheldt at Antwerp. King Henry beneath the Oak of Justice, with Counts and Nobles from the Saxon militia beside him. Opposite them are the Brabantine Counts and Nobles, headed by Frederick of Telramund, with Ortrud at his side. The Herald steps forth from the King's militia and moves towards the centre of the stage: at a signal from him, four of the King's trumpeters issue a call to arms.* [3]

HERALD

Hear, princes, nobles, freemen of Brabant!	Hört! Grafen, Edle, Freie von Brabant!
Henry the king of Germany has arrived	Heinrich, der Deutschen König, kam zur Statt
to speak with you according to the law.	mit euch zu dingen nach des Reiches Recht.
Do you agree to follow his command?	Gebt ihr nun Fried' und Folge dem Gebot?

THE BRABANTINES

Yes, we agree to follow his command!	Wir geben Fried' und Folge dem Gebot.

(striking their weapons together)

We welcome, we welcome Henry to Brabant!	Willkommen! Willkommen, König, in Brabant!

KING HENRY
(rising)

God bless you, worthy people of Brabant!	Gott grüss' euch, liebe Männer von Brabant!

(freely declaimed)

I travelled here to bring important news;	Nicht müssig that zu euch ich diese Fahrt;

(very emphatically)

I've come to remind you of our country's plight.	der Noth des Reiches seid von mir gemahnt.

(Solemn attention all round.)

But first we must remember all the dangers	Soll ich euch erst der Drangsal Kunde sagen,
so often faced by Germany from the East.	die deutsches Land so oft aus Osten traf?
This was the prayer of all your wives and children:	In fernster Mark heiss't Weib und Kind ihr beten:
'Save us, o God, from the Hungarian hordes!'	Herr Gott, bewahr' uns vor der Ungarn Wuth!
As king and head of state, it was my duty	Doch mir, des Reiches Haupt, musst' es geziemen
to go to war and end this dreadful menace.	solch wilder Schmach ein Ende zu ersinnen:
My victory ensured our freedom for	als Kampfes Preis gewann ich Frieden auf
nine years, I used them for the realm's defence.	neun Jahr', ihn nützt' ich zu des Reiches Wehr;
I had our towns and castles reinforced	beschirmte Städt' und Burgen liess ich bau'n,
and built our armies up to greater strength.	den Heerbann übte ich zum Widerstand.
But peace is at an end, and once again	Zu End' ist nun die Frist, der Zins versagt,
the fierce Hungarians threaten us with war.	mit wildem Drohen rüstet sich der Feind.

Now is the time to fight for king and
country;
from East to West all must prepare for
war!
Throughout our kingdom men must
take up weapons;
they'll be destroyed and gone for
evermore!

Nun ist es Zeit des Reiches Ehr' zu
wahren;
ob Ost, ob West, das gelte Allen gleich!
Was deutsches Land heisst, stelle
Kampfesschaaren,
dann schmäht wohl Niemand mehr das
deutsche Reich!

THE SAXONS
(striking their weapons together)

Protect the honour of our land!
With God we'll save our land!

Wohlauf für deutschen Reiches Ehr'!
Mit Gott für Reiches Ehr'!

KING HENRY

These are your orders, soldiers of
Brabant,
to go to Mainz to join there with my
army.
But I am grieved to find you not at
peace,
that, since no leader governs, discord
reigns!
Confusion, feuds and factions have been
rife.
I call on you, Frederick of Telramund.

I know you are a man whom I can trust:
you tell me, what's the reason for the
strife?

Komm' ich zu euch nun, Männer von
Brabant,
zur Heeresfolg' nach Mainz euch zu
entbieten,
wie muss mit Schmerz und Klagen ich
erseh'n,
dass ohne Fürsten ihr in Zwietracht
lebt!
Verwirrung, wilde Fehde wird mir
kund;
drum ruf' ich dich, Friedrich von
Telramund:
ich kenne dich als aller Tugend Preis,
jetzt rede, dass der Drangsal Grund
ich weiss.

FREDERICK

Thank you, my lord, your judgement's
welcome here!
I shall be truthful, I could never lie.

Before his death the Duke of Brabant

appointed me the guardian of his
children,
Elsa, his daughter, and Godfrey, her
brother.
I loved the boy as if he were my own son,

that child was all my joy and all I lived
for.
Imagine, Highness, my distress and grief

when he I loved so dearly was snatched
away.
One day he went with Elsa walking
in the woods, when she returned she
was alone;
naively asking if I'd seen her brother,

she said they'd lost each other by
mistake;
she'd looked and looked, so she
said, but he was gone.
Futile and vain were all attempts to find
him,
and when I pressed his sister for the
truth,
she, pale and trembling, petrified and
shaking,

Dank, König, dir, dass du zu richten
kamst!
Die Wahrheit künd' ich, Untreu' ist
mir fremd.
Zum Sterben kam der Herzog von
Brabant,
und meinem Schutz empfahl er seine
Kinder,
Elsa, die Jungfrau, und Gottfried, den
Knaben:
mit Treue pflag ich seiner grossen
Jugend,
sein Leben war das Kleinod meiner
Ehre.
Ermiss nun, König, meinen grimmen
Schmerz,
als meiner Ehre Kleinod mir geraubt!

Lustwandelnd führte Elsa den Knaben
einst zum Wald, doch ohne ihn kehrte
sie zurück;
mit falscher Sorge frug sie nach dem
Bruder,
da sie, von ungefähr von ihm verirrt,

bald seine Spur — so sprach sie —
nicht mehr fand.
Fruchtlos war all' Bemüh'n um den
Verlor'nen;
als ich mit Drohen nun in Elsa drang,

da liess in bleichem Zagen und Erbeben

all but confessed to us her dreadful crime.
At once I felt revulsion for the girl.
Her father's dying wish that she should marry me I then declined with great relief,
and took a wife more worthy of my love:

der grässlichen Schuld Bekenntniss sie uns seh'n.
Es fasste mich Entsetzen vor der Magd:
dem Recht auf ihre Hand, vom Vater mir verlieh'n, entsagt' ich willig da und gern,
und nahm ein Weib, das meinem Sinn gefiel,

(He presents Ortrud, who acknowledges the King with a nod of her head.)

Ortrud, daughter of Radbod, Friesland's prince.

Ortrud, Radbod's des Friesenfürsten Spross.

(He solemnly advances a few paces.) [4]

I bring this charge against Elsa of Brabant: her brother's murder is her crime.
I claim this land as mine to rule by right,
for after Elsa I am next in line,
and my wife's descended from the house that gave
Brabant its ancient royal dynasty.
You've heard the truth, Your Highness! You must judge!

Nun führ' ich Klage wider Elsa von Brabant: des Brudermordes zeih' ich sie.
Diess Land doch sprech' ich für mich an mit Recht,
da ich der Nächste von des Herzog's Blut,
mein Weib dazu aus dem Geschlecht, das einst
auch diesen Landen seine Fürsten gab.
Du hörst die Klage, König! Richte recht!

ALL THE MEN
(with solemn dread)

Ah! Telramund, what a dreadful thing,
to charge Elsa before the king!

Ha, schwerer Schuld zeiht Telramund!
Mit Grau'n werd' ich der Klage kund.

KING HENRY

A fearful accusation has been made!

Welch' fürchterliche Klage sprichst du aus!

Could she have done this, such a gruesome crime?

Wie wäre möglich solche grosse Schuld?

FREDERICK
(increasingly vehemently)

But Sire! She is deluded by her dreams, in pride she spurned the offer of my hand.
I know that Elsa has a secret love

O Herr, traumselig ist die eitle Magd, die meine Hand voll Hochmuth von sich stiess.
Geheimer Buhlschaft klag' ich drum sie an:

(betraying increasingly bitter exasperation)

and clearly thought that if she killed her brother,
she, by becoming Duchess of Brabant, could then refuse me as her rightful husband
and live openly with her secret lover.

sie wähnte wohl, wenn sie des Bruders ledig,
dann könnte sie als Herrin von Brabant mit Recht dem Lehnsmann ihre Hand verwehren,
und offen des geheimen Buhlen pflegen.

With a grave gesture the King interrupts Frederick's impassioned account.

KING HENRY
(very solemnly)

Let the accused be called! The trial commences
here at once! God make me wise and strong!

Ruft die Beklagte her! Beginnen soll
nun das Gericht! Gott lass' mich weise sein!

The Herald solemnly advances to the centre of the stage.

HERALD

Here may the trial be held according to the law?

Soll hier nach Recht und Macht Gericht gehalten sein?

The King solemnly hangs his shield on the oak.

51

KING HENRY

My shield shall not go forth to fight
until we know the judgement's right!

Nicht eh'r soll bergen mich der Schild
bis ich gerichtet streng und mild!

All the men unsheathe their swords; the Saxons thrust theirs into the ground in front of them, while the Brabantines lay theirs flat on the ground before them.

ALL THE MEN

The scabbard shall not hold the sword
until our peace has been restored.

Nicht eh'r zur Scheide kehr' das Schwert
bis ihm durch Urtheil Recht gewährt!

HERALD

This place shall hold the royal shield
until the truth has been revealed.
I make the summons loud and clear:
Elsa, you must attend us here!

Wo ihr des Königs Schild gewahrt,
dort Recht und Urtheil nun erfahrt!
Drum ruf' ich klagend laut und hell:
Elsa, erscheine hier zur Stell'!

Scene Two. *Elsa enters; she lingers for a moment at the back, then with great modesty moves very slowly downstage; women follow her but initially remain in the background, at the extreme edge of the judgement circle.* [5]

ALL THE MEN

She's here! She's come to face the charges!

Seht hin! Sie naht, die hart Beklagte!

[6]

Ah! She approaches so fair and pure!
If he dares make such accusations,
then of her guilt he must be sure.

Ha, wie erscheint sie so licht und rein!
Der sie so schwer zu zeihen wagte,
wie sicher muss der Schuld er sein.

KING HENRY

Your name is Elsa of Brabant?

Bist du es, Elsa von Brabant?

(Elsa inclines her head in affirmation.)

Do you accept that I may judge your case?

Erkennst du mich als deinen Richter an?

(Elsa turns her head towards the King, looks into his eyes and, with a gesture of trust, nods her agreement.)

Then I will continue: tell me this, are you aware
that you have been accused of murder?

So frage ich weiter: ist die Klage dir bekannt,
die schwer hier wider dich erhoben?

(Elsa catches sight of Frederick and Ortrud, sadly lowers her head and gestures her assent.)

What's your answer to the question?

Was entgegnest du der Klage?

(Elsa gestures, as if to say 'Nothing'.)

Are you guilty of the crime?

So bekennst du deine Schuld?

Elsa gazes sadly in front of her for a moment.

ELSA

My poor dear brother!

Mein armer Bruder!

THE MEN
(whispering)

How curious, how strange is her behaviour!

Wie wunderbar! Welch' seltsames Gebaren!

KING HENRY
(moved)

Speak, Elsa! Have you nothing to confess?

Sag', Elsa! Was hast du mir zu vertrau'n?

Expectant silence.

When all my hopes departed	[7]	Einsam in trüben Tagen
God kept me from despair;		hab' ich zu Gott gefleht,
alone and broken-hearted,		des Herzens tiefstes Klagen
I turned to him in prayer.		ergoss ich im Gebet.
And from my groans of anguish		Da drang aus meinem Stöhnen
a cry of pain did rise,		ein Laut so klagevoll,
surging with mighty power,		der zu gewalt'gem Tönen
soaring above to the skies:		weit in die Lüfte schwoll:
I heard the distant echo		ich hört' ihn fern hin hallen,
and ceased at once to weep;		bis kaum mein Ohr er traf;
I closed my weary eyelids		mein Aug' ist zugefallen,
and drifted into sleep.		ich sank in süssen Schlaf.

[handwritten: big rise]

ALL THE MEN

Mysterious! She's dreaming? Is she bewitched?

Wie sonderbar! Träumt sie? Ist sie entrückt?

KING HENRY
(as though seeking to rouse Elsa from her reverie)

Elsa, defend yourself before the court!

Elsa, vertheid'ge dich vor dem Gericht!

Elsa's expression changes from dreamy ecstasy to rapturous transfiguration.

ELSA *[handwritten: ~ Lohengrin / heavenly part]*

A knight in shining armour	In lichter Waffen Scheine
appeared before my eyes;	ein Ritter nahte da,
I never saw such virtue,	so tugendlicher Reine
he looked so fair and wise.	ich keinen noch ersah.
A golden horn beside him,	Ein golden Horn zur Hüften,
he leant upon a sword.	gelehnet auf sein Schwert,
Thus he appeared from Heaven,	so trat er aus den Lüften
my faithful warrior lord.	zu mir, der Recke werth.
The comfort that he gave me	Mit züchtigem Gebaren
has eased my fear and shame;	gab Tröstung er mir ein:

(raising her voice)

I know that he will save me,

des Ritters will ich wahren,

(rapturously)

he will defend my name!

er soll mein Streiter sein!

[handwritten: he shall be my champion]

ALL THE MEN
(deeply moved)

May Heaven make its judgement clear that we may know who's guilty here.

Bewahre uns des Himmels Huld, dass klar wir sehen, wer hier schuld!

KING HENRY

Frederick, you are an honest man,

Friedrich, du ehrenwerther Mann,

(more animatedly)

consider well whom you accuse.

bedenke wohl, wen klagst du an?

FREDERICK

I won't be fooled by fairytales and dreams;	Mich irret nicht ihr träumerischer Muth;

(increasingly impassioned)

you heard, she raves about a lover!	ihr hört, sie schwärmt von einem Buhlen!
I've valid grounds, that's why I brought the charge:	Wess' ich sie zeih', dess' hab' ich sich'ren Grund;
proof of her guilt was testified to me.	glaubwürdig ward ihr Frevel mir bezeugt.
But do not ask me to present my witness:	Doch eurem Zweifel durch ein Zeugniss wehren,
that would insult my dignity and pride.	das stünde wahrlich übel meinem Stolz!
I'm ready, here's my sword! Which one of you	Hier steh' ich, hier mein Schwert! Wer wagt von euch
will dare to challenge me in honour's name?	zu streiten wider meiner Ehre Preis?

THE BRABANTINE NOBLES
(very animatedly)

Not one of us! We'll only fight for you!	Keiner von uns! Wir streiten nur für dich.

FREDERICK

And you, my king! You surely still remember how I won victory against the Danes?	Und, König, du! Gedenkst du meiner Dienste, wie ich im Kampf den wilden Dänen schlug?

KING HENRY
(animatedly)

Indeed! How could I ever forget it?	Wie schlimm, liess' ich von dir daran mich mahnen!
You are a man I hold in high esteem;	Gern geb' ich dir der höchsten Tugend Preis;
there's no one else but you by whom I'd rather	in keiner and'ren Huth, als in der deinen
see Brabant protected. God alone	möcht' ich die Lande wissen. Gott allein

(with solemn resolve)

will make the final judgement in this matter.	soll jetzt in dieser Sache noch entscheiden!

ALL THE MEN

Let God be the judge! Let God be the judge! Agreed!	Zum Gottesgericht! Zum Gottesgericht! Wohlan!

The King draws his sword and thrusts it into the ground in front of him. [9]

KING HENRY

I ask you, Frederick, Count of Telramund: do you agree to fight unto the death in God's holy sight to prove your accusation?	Dich frag' ich, Friedrich, Graf von Telramund! Willst du durch Kampf auf Leben und auf Tod im Gottesgericht vertreten deine Klage?

FREDERICK

Yes!	Ja!

KING HENRY

Now you must answer, Elsa of Brabant! Do you agree that combat may be fought in God's holy sight by one you name as champion?	Und dich nun frag' ich, Elsa von Brabant! Willst du, dass hier auf Leben und auf Tod im Gottesgericht ein Kämpe für dich streite?

ELSA
(without raising her eyes)

Yes!	Ja!

KING HENRY

Whom do you choose as champion?	Wen wählest du zum Streiter?

FREDERICK
(quickly)

Now we will learn the name of her secret lover!	Vernehmet jetzt den Namen ihres Buhlen!

THE BRABANTINE NOBLES

What's his name?	Merket auf!

Elsa's attitude and rapt expression remain unchanged; all look at her expectantly.

ELSA
(firmly)

My knight will be my champion	Des Ritters will ich wahren,
and he will fight for me!	er soll mein Streiter sein!

(without looking round)

Hear what reward I offer	Hört, was dem Gottgesandten
the man whom God will send,	ich biete zu Gewähr:
for in my father's country	in meines Vaters Landen
the throne he shall ascend;	die Krone trage er;
it is my fond ambition	mich glücklich soll ich preisen,
to offer him my life;	nimmt er mein Gut dahin,
if he will come to save me,	will er Gemahl mich heissen,

(slowly)

I'll gladly be his wife!	geb' ich ihm was ich bin!

ALL THE MEN
(aside)

A wondrous prize, if it were God's reward,	Ein schöner Preis, stünd' er in Gottes Hand!

(to each other)

but he who fights may perish by the sword!	Wer um ihn stritt, wohl setzt' er schweres Pfand.

KING HENRY

The midday sun shines high above us,	Im Mittag hoch steht schon die Sonne:
now is the time to call the champion here.	so ist es Zeit, dass nun der Ruf ergeh'.

The Herald advances with the four trumpeters, whom he directs to stand at the extreme edge of the judgement circle, facing the four cardinal points, and to blow their call from there.

HERALD

He who will come to fight as champion	Wer hier im Gotteskampf zu streiten kam
for Elsa of Brabant, let him appear!	für Elsa von Brabant, der trete vor!

Elsa has remained calm hitherto, but now shows increasing signs of disquiet.

ALL THE MEN

The call echoes and dies away!	Ohn' Antwort ist der Ruf verhallt:
It seems for Elsa hope has died.	um ihre Sache steht es schlecht.

FREDERICK
(pointing to Elsa)

You see, how can my charge be false?	Gewahrt, ob ich sie fälschlich schalt:
For I have justice on my side.	auf meiner Seite bleibt das Recht.

ELSA
(coming somewhat closer to the King)

Your Royal Highness, I beseech you,	Mein lieber König, lass dich bitten,
send one more call to my defender.	noch einen Ruf an meinen Ritter!

(very innocently)

He's far away and did not hear.	Wohl weilt er fern und hört' ihn nicht.

KING HENRY
(to the Herald)

Once more command him to appear!	Noch einmal rufe zum Gericht!

At a sign from the Herald, the four trumpeters once again face the four cardinal points.

HERALD

He who will come to fight as champion	Wer hier im Gotteskampf zu streiten kam
for Elsa of Brabant, let him appear!	für Elsa von Brabant, der trete vor!

With total silence God responds.	In düst'rem Schweigen richtet Gott.

Elsa sinks to her knees in fervent prayer. In their concern for their mistress, her womenfolk come somewhat further downstage.

ELSA

God, you revealed to him my sorrow;	Du trugest zu ihm meine Klage,
he came to me at your behest.	zu mir trat er auf dein Gebot;
O God, call to my knight and tell him,	o Herr, nun meinem Ritter sage,
I need his help in my distress.	dass er mir helf' in meiner Noth!

(with growing inspiration)

Just as before make him appear;	Lass mich ihn seh'n wie ich ihn sah,

(with an expression of joyful transfiguration)

make him appear, ah, send him here!	wie ich ihn sah sei er mir nah'!

WOMEN
(falling on their knees)

God, send a champion here! Lord God, hear us!	Herr! Sende Hülfe ihr! Herr Gott! höre uns!

The First Chorus consists of the men standing closest to the water's edge; they are the first to see Lohengrin arrive, as he comes into sight in the distance on the river in a skiff drawn by a swan. The Second Chorus is made up of those more remote from the water's edge who, without initially abandoning their positions, turn to those standing closer to the water's edge and question them with increasing inquisitiveness, before moving upstage in individual groups in order to see for themselves. [8]

MEN

Look! Look! A mysterious wonder!	Seht! seht! welch' ein seltsam Wunder!
What? A swan?	Wie? Ein Schwan,
A swan pulling a boat towards the shore!	ein Schwan zieht einen Nachen dort heran!
A knight is there, he's standing in the boat!	Ein Ritter drin hoch aufgerichtet steht;
His armour's glittering! My eyes are dazzled	wie glänzt sein Waffenschmuck! Das Aug' vergeht
by the light! Look! He is almost here!	vor solchem Glanz! Seht näher kommt er an!

At this point Lohengrin disappears from the audience's gaze behind a group of trees on a bend in the river, although the singers can still see him approaching off-stage right. All have now rushed to the back of the stage, so that only the King, Elsa, Frederick, Ortrud and the womenfolk remain downstage.

The swan is pulling on a golden chain!	An einer gold'nen Kette zieht der Schwan!

All rush to the front of the stage in the utmost excitement. The King observes events unfolding from his elevated position; Frederick and Ortrud are rooted to the spot in terror and astonishment; Elsa, who has listened to the men's shouts with mounting joy, remains where she is in the middle of the stage, not daring to look round.

Scene Three.

MEN

A wonder! A wonder! A miracle has happened,	Ein Wunder! Ein Wunder! Ein Wunder ist gekommen!
an overwhelming, strange, unheard-of wonder!	Ein unerhörtes, nie geseh'nes Wunder!

WOMEN
(sinking to their knees)

Thank you, Lord and God, for protecting this woman!	Dank, du Herr und Gott, der die Schwache beschirmet!

All eyes are now turned expectantly upstage.

ELSA

Ah!   Ah!

MEN AND WOMEN

We greet you, hero sent by God!   Gegrüsst! Gegrüsst, du gottgesandter
                                       Held!

*By now the swan-drawn skiff has reached the shore upstage centre; in it stands Lohengrin in
gleaming silver armour, helmet on head, a shield at his back and a small golden horn at his side;
he is leaning on his sword. Frederick stares at Lohengrin in speechless astonishment; Ortrud, who
had preserved a cold, haughty demeanour during the trial, is struck by deathly terror at the sight
of the swan. All bare their heads in profound emotion. At this point Elsa turns round and cries
out aloud on seeing Lohengrin. As Lohengrin makes a move to step out of the skiff, the most intense
silence descends over the scene.*

LOHENGRIN
(with one foot still in the boat, bending towards the swan)

I thank you, beloved friend!   [10] Nun sei bedankt, mein lieber Schwan!
Over the water glide away,   Zieh’ durch die weite Fluth zurück
go back to the horizon’s end,   dahin, woher mich trug dein Kahn,
never return until the day   kehr’ wieder nur zu uns’rem Glück!
you bring us joy and sorrow is gone!   Drum sei getreu dein Dienst gethan!
*(The swan slowly turns the skiff round and swims back upstream. Lohengrin gazes sadly after
it for a while.)*
Farewell, farewell, beloved swan!   Leb’ wohl, leb’ wohl, mein lieber
                                       Schwan!

MEN AND WOMEN

What sense of wonder overcomes us!   [11] Wie fasst uns selig süsses Grauen!
What power holds us in its hand?   Welch’ holde Macht hält uns gebannt!
(At this point Lohengrin leaves the water’s edge and moves slowly and solemnly downstage.)
He is so fine, so fair and noble,   Wie ist er schön und hehr zu schauen,
brought here by magic to our land!   den solch’ ein Wunder trug an’s Land!

LOHENGRIN
(bowing to the King)

Greetings, Your Highness! Blest are you   Heil König Heinrich! Segenvoll
whom God appoints to keep His law.   mög’ Gott bei deinem Schwerte steh’n!
All through the world your name shall be   Ruhmreich und gross dein Name soll
revered and honoured evermore!   von dieser Erde nie vergeh’n!

KING HENRY

My thanks! I think I know what   Hab’ Dank! Erkenn’ ich recht die Macht,
awesome power has brought you to this   die dich in dieses Land gebracht,
   land.
Have you been sent to us by God?   so nahst du uns von Gott gesandt?

LOHENGRIN

To stand and fight for one who claims   Zum Kampf für eine Magd zu steh’n,
that she is wrongfully accused,   der schwere Klage angethan,
that’s why I’m sent: now I shall see   bin ich gesandt: nun lasst mich seh’n,
if I was right to heed her call.   ob ich zurecht sie treffe an!
(turning more towards Elsa)
So tell me, Elsa of Brabant!   So sprich denn, Elsa von Brabant!
If as your champion I appear,   Wenn ich zum Streiter dir ernannt,
will you trust me with heart and soul,   willst du wohl ohne Bang’ und Grau’n
trust my protection without fear?   dich meinem Schutze anvertrau’n?

*Since catching sight of Lohengrin, Elsa had remained motionless, as if spell-bound, but she now
seems to wake up on being addressed by him and sinks at his feet, overwhelmed by her feelings of
joy.*

ELSA

My knight, my saviour, I am yours!   Mein Held, mein Retter! Nimm mich
                                       hin!

Yes, I will trust you evermore!   Dir geb’ ich alles was ich bin!

LOHENGRIN
(with greater warmth)

If I'm victorious in the contest, will you agree to marry me?	Wenn ich im Kampfe für dich siege, willst du, dass ich dein Gatte sei?

ELSA

You do not need to ask the question: loving and faithful I shall be!	Wie ich zu deinen Füssen liege, geb' ich dir Leib und Seele frei.

LOHENGRIN

Elsa, if I become your husband, if I'm to set your people free, if nothing is to tear me from you, to this demand you must agree.	Elsa, soll ich dein Gatte heissen, soll Land und Leut' ich schirmen dir, soll nichts mich wieder von dir reissen, musst Eines du geloben mir:

(very slowly)

My history is hidden, these questions are forbidden: to ask from whence I came or seek to know my name.	[12]	nie sollst du mich befragen, noch Wissen's Sorge tragen, woher ich kam der Fahrt, noch wie mein Nam' und Art!

ELSA
(quietly, almost unconsciously)

I promise I shall never ask you!	Nie, Herr, soll mir die Frage kommen.

LOHENGRIN
(intensely and with great seriousness)

Elsa! Do you understand me?	Elsa! Hast du mich wohl vernommen?

(even more emphatically)

My history is hidden, these questions are forbidden: to ask from whence I came or seek to know my name.	Nie sollst du mich befragen, noch Wissen's Sorge tragen, woher ich kam der Fahrt, noch wie mein Nam' und Art!

ELSA
(looking up at him with great inwardness)

My love, my angel, my protector! Since you believe me free from blame, why should I ever want to hurt you, to disobey and ask your name? As you're protecting me from harm, so I shall honour your command.	Mein Schirm! Mein Engel! Mein Erlöser der fest an meine Unschuld glaubt! Wie gäb' es Zweifels Schuld, die grösser, als die an dich den Glauben raubt? Wie du mich schirmst in meiner Noth, so halt' in Treu ich dein Gebot.

LOHENGRIN
(raising Elsa to his breast)

Elsa, I love you!	Elsa, ich liebe dich!

Both remain in this position for a moment, then Lohengrin leads Elsa to the King and gives her into his care.

MEN AND WOMEN
(softly and with emotion)

What blissful wonder have I seen? What magic spell is cast on me? I am at peace within my soul when I behold this gentle, saintly man.	Welch' holde Wunder muss ich seh'n? Ist's Zauber, der mir angethan? Ich fühl' das Herz mir vergeh'n, schau' ich den hehren, wonnevollen Mann.

Lohengrin steps solemnly into the centre of the circle.

LOHENGRIN

And now! Listen, you people of Brabant: Elsa is pure and innocent of blame!	Nun hört! Euch Volk und Edlen mach' ich kund: frei aller Schuld ist Elsa von Brabant.

Your claim's a false one, Count of
Telramund.
Now God shall judge you and restore
her name!

Dass falsch dein Klagen, Graf von
Telramund,
durch Gottes Urtheil werd' es dir
bekannt!

You must not fight! Once you begin

you cannot ever hope to win.
He is protected from above,
even your sword will be no use.

Stay out! We urge you to desist!
Failure awaits you, don't insist!

Steh' ab vom Kampf! wenn du ihn
wagst,
zu siegen nimmer du vermagst!
Ist er von höchster Macht geschützt,
sag', was dein tapf'res Schwert dir
nützt?
Steh' ab! Wir mahnen dich in Treu'!
Dein harret Unsieg, bitt're Reu'!

FREDERICK
(who has kept his eyes fixed inquiringly on Lohengrin)
(forcefully)

I am resolved: I'll fight!
Whatever magic brought you here,
stranger, to boldly take her side,
I won't be daunted by your threats,

because I know I never lied.
I'll fight with you till my last breath;

God is our judge in life or death!

Viel lieber todt als feig!
Welch' Zaubern dich auch hergeführt,
Fremdling, der mir so kühn erscheint,
dein stolzes Droh'n mich nimmer
rührt,
da ich zu lügen nie vermeint.
Den Kampf mit dir drum nehm' ich
auf,
und hoffe Sieg nach Rechtes Lauf!

LOHENGRIN

So be it! Let the fight begin!

Nun, König, ord'ne uns'ren Kampf!

All resume their positions at the beginning of the trial.

KING HENRY

We need three men to second each
contestant,
and measure out the circle for the fight!

So tretet vor, zu drei für jeden
Kämpfer,
und messet wohl den Ring zum Streite
ab!

*Three Saxon nobles step forward for Lohengrin, three Brabantine nobles for Frederick. They
solemnly cross the stage and measure out the field of combat. Having formed a complete circle,
all six of them then thrust their spears into the ground.*

HERALD
(in the centre of the circle)

Now I remind you of the law:
the combat must not be disturbed
and all must stay outside the ring.
He who ignores what I have said,

if freeman he shall lose his hand
and if a serf he forfeits his head!

Nun höret mich, und achtet wohl:
den Kampf hier keiner stören soll!
Dem Hage bleibet abgewandt,
denn wer nicht wahrt des Friedens
Recht,
der Freie büss' es mit der Hand,
mit seinem Haupte büss' es der Knecht!

ALL THE MEN

The freeman, he shall lose his hand
and if a serf he forfeits his head!

Der Freie büss' es mit der Hand,
mit seinem Haupte büss' es der Knecht!

HERALD

And you who fight before your God,
you must respect the rules of war!
Let no deceit or guile or hate
seek to destroy God's awesome might!
Heaven alone decides your fate,
with trust in God prepare to fight!

Hört auch, ihr Streiter vor Gericht!
Gewahrt in Treue Kampfespflicht!
Durch bösen Zaubers List und Trug
stört nicht des Urtheils Eigenschaft!
Gott richtet euch nach Recht und Fug,
so trauet ihm, nicht eurer Kraft!

Heaven alone decides my fate,	Gott richte mich nach Recht und Fug,
with trust in God I dare to fight!	so trau' ich ihm, nicht meiner Kraft!

The King advances to the centre of the circle with great solemnity.

KING HENRY

My Lord and God, I pray to you:	[13] Mein Herr und Gott, nun ruf' ich dich,

(All bare their heads in an attitude of the most solemn devotion.)

may you be present at this fight,	dass du dem Kampf zugegen sei'st!
that through the sword your judgement speaks	Durch Schwertes Sieg ein Urtheil sprich,
and shows us clearly who is right!	das Trug und Wahrheit klar erweis't.
Give him who's blameless a hero's strength	Des Reinen Arm gieb Heldenkraft,
and make the one who's guilty weak.	des Falschen Stärke sei erschlafft:
So help us, God, for we are frail.	so hilf uns, Gott, zu dieser Frist,
We know your justice will prevail.	weil uns're Weisheit Einfalt ist!

ELSA AND LOHENGRIN

I know you'll make your judgement clear,	Du kündest nun dein wahr Gericht,
my Lord and God, I shall not fear.	mein Herr und Gott, drum zag' ich nicht.

FREDERICK

I come before your judgement here,	Ich geh' in Treu' vor dein Gericht:
Lord God, give me strength to persevere!	Herr Gott, verlass' mein' Ehre nicht!

ORTRUD

He'll win, I know, I am not wrong,	Ich baue fest auf seine Kraft,
for he is brave and he is strong.	die, wo er kämpft, ihm Sieg verschafft.

ALL THE MEN

Give him who's blameless a hero's strength	Des Reinen Arm gieb Heldenkraft,
and make the man who's guilty weak.	des Falschen Stärke sei erschlafft:
So help us, God, for we are frail.	so hilf uns, Gott, zu dieser Frist,
We know your justice will prevail.	weil uns're Weisheit Einfalt ist!
We know you'll make your judgement clear,	So künde uns dein wahr Gericht,
my Lord and God, I shall not fear!	du Herr und Gott, nun zög're nicht!

WOMEN

My Lord and God! Stay with him!	Mein Herr und Gott! Segne ihn!

All return to their places in a state of deep but solemn excitement; the six witnesses initially remain standing by their spears at the edge of the ring, with the rest of the men encircling them. Elsa and her women at the front of the stage, next to the King, beneath the oak. At a sign from the Herald, the trumpeters issue a call to battle. Lohengrin and Frederick finish arming themselves. The King draws his sword from the ground and strikes three blows with it against his shield, which is still hanging from the oak tree. At the first blow, Lohengrin and Frederick enter the lists; at the second, they raise their shields and draw their swords; and at the third, they begin fighting. Lohengrin is the first to attack. He fells Frederick with a mighty stroke. Frederick attempts to get up, staggers a few paces backwards and falls to the ground.

LOHENGRIN
(placing his sword on Frederick's neck)

Our God decrees that victory is mine:	Durch Gottes Sieg ist jetzt dein Leben mein:

(releasing him)

I spare your life, go and repent in peace!	ich schenk' es dir! mög'st du der Reu' es weih'n!

All the men reclaim their swords and return them to their scabbards; the witnesses draw their spears
out of the ground, and the King takes down his shield from the oak. All crowd joyfully to the centre
of the stage and in doing so cover the area previously used for the combat. Elsa hurries over to
Lohengrin. The King, too, thrusts his sword back into its scabbard.

MEN AND WOMEN

Hail! Hail! Hail, all hail!   Sieg! Sieg! Heil! Heil dir, Held!

ELSA

Oh, could I find the words [14]   O fänd' ich Jubelweisen,
to celebrate and raise   deinem Ruhme gleich,
a song of glory,   dich würdig zu preisen,
of gladness and of praise!   an höchstem Lobe reich!
We'll always be together,   In dir muss ich vergehen,
of you I am a part!   vor dir schwind' ich dahin!
Let me be yours for ever,   Soll ich mich selig sehen,
oh, take me to your heart!   nimm alles was ich bin!

She sinks upon Lohengrin's breast.

LOHENGRIN
(raising Elsa from his breast)

Your faith has been rewarded   Den Sieg hab' ich erstritten
and God has cleared your name.   durch deine Rein' allein!
Now you shall be awarded   nun soll, was du gelitten,
a life that's free of shame.   dir reich vergolten sein!

FREDERICK

I am by God forsaken,   Weh'! mich hat Gott geschlagen,
by him condemned to shame.   durch ihn ich sieglos bin!
The judgement is mistaken!   Am Heil muss ich versagen,
He has destroyed my name!   mein Ruhm und Ehr' ist hin!

ORTRUD
(gazing darkly and fixedly at Lohengrin)

Who's this, this man who beat him,   Wer ist's, der ihn geschlagen,
by whom my strength is drained?   vor dem ich machtlos bin?
Unless I can defeat him,   Sollt' ich vor ihm verzagen,
my hopes will be in vain.   wär' all' mein Hoffen hin?

KING HENRY, MEN AND WOMEN

Hosanna! Sing out proudly   Ertöne, Siegesweise,
and praise the hero loudly!   dem Helden laut zum Preise!
   Praise to your sword,   Ruhm deiner Fahrt!
   saviour from Heaven!   Preis deinem Kommen!
   Hear us applaud,   Heil deiner Art,
   stay here for ever!   Schützer der Frommen!
(with the utmost enthusiasm)
You answered Elsa's call,   Dich nur besingen wir,
you fought for her and freed her!   dir schallen unsre Lieder!
God sent you here to us   Nie kehrt ein Held gleich dir
and you shall be our leader!   zu diesen Landen wieder!

Young men raise Lohengrin on his shield and Elsa on the King's, having first spread their mantles
over it; both are carried off amid shouts of rejoicing. Frederick falls senseless at Ortrud's feet.

The curtain falls.

Above: Ann Howard as Ortrud and Raimund Herincx as Telramund in the 1971 Sadler's Wells production (photo: John Garner)

Below: Alberto Remedios as Lohengrin and Margaret Curphey as Elsa, Sadler's Wells at the London Coliseum, 1971 (photo: Zoë Dominic)

Act Two

Scene One. *The curtain rises. The scene is the castle at Antwerp, with the banqueting hall in the background, the 'Kemenate' (women's quarters) downstage left, and the Minster on the right. It is night. Ortrud and Frederick, both in dark, servile apparel, are sitting on the Minster steps, Frederick gloomily introspective, while Ortrud gazes fixedly at the brightly lit windows of the banqueting hall, from which festive music can be heard.* [15]

FREDERICK
(rising suddenly)

Arouse yourself, our exile has begun!
When morning comes, they must not
find us here.

Erhebe dich, Genossin meiner Schmach!
Der junge Tag darf hier uns nicht mehr
seh'n.

ORTRUD
(without changing her position)

I cannot go, I'm held here by a spell.

The sight of their rejoicing feeds my
anger
and fills my soul with bitter deadly hate;

I'll end our shame and wreck their joy
for ever!

Ich kann nicht fort: hieher bin ich
gebannt.
Aus diesem Glanz des Festes unsres
Feindes,
lass saugen mich ein furchtbar tödtlich
Gift,
dass unsre Schmach und ihre Freuden
ende!

FREDERICK
(standing darkly before Ortrud)

You dark and fearsome woman! What is
it keeps
me here beside you?

Du fürchterliches Weib! Was bannt mich
noch
in deine Nähe?

(with rapidly increasing violence)

      And why can't I abandon you
and go away, away, away,

      Warum lass' ich dich nicht
allein, und fliehe fort, dahin, dahin,

(with anguish)

and let my guilty conscience rest in
peace?

wo mein Gewissen Ruhe wieder fänd'?

(with the most violent outburst of painful passion and rage)

It's you who have destroyed me,
I'm lost, I am bereft;
honour and fame avoid me,
shame is what I have left!
My glorious name has vanished,
my sword torn from my hands.
Condemned, despised and banished,
I've lost my fatherland!
Wherever life may lead me,
pursued by scorn and hate,
dishonour will precede me,
shame is my dreadful fate!

Durch dich musst' ich verlieren
mein' Ehr', all' meinen Ruhm:
nie soll mich Lob mehr zieren,
Schmach ist mein Heldenthum!
Die Acht ist mir gesprochen,
zertrümmert liegt mein Schwert;
mein Wappen ward zerbrochen,
verflucht mein Vaterherd!
Wohin ich nun mich wende,
gebannt, gefehmt bin ich:
dass ihn mein Blick nicht schände,
flieht selbst der Räuber mich.

(almost in tears)

Would I had died in combat
and so relieved this pain!

O hätt' ich Tod erkoren,
da ich so elend bin!

(in utter despair)

I'm lost and you've condemned me
to live, to live in shame.

mein' Ehr' hab' ich verloren,
mein' Ehr', mein' Ehr' ist hin!

He falls to the ground, overwhelmed by rage and anguish.
Music is heard from the banqueting hall.

ORTRUD
(still in the same position, as Frederick rises to his feet)

What's causing all this wild resentment
and
this rage?

Was macht dich in so wilder Klage doch

vergeh'n?

63

FREDERICK

Because I've even lost my sword   Dass mir die Waffe selbst geraubt,
(with a violent gesture)
and cannot strike you dead!   mit der ich dich erschlüg'!

ORTRUD
(with calm contempt)

Dear, loving Count   Friedreicher Graf
of Telramund! Have you no trust in me?   von Telramund! Weshalb mistrau'st du
    mir?

FREDERICK

You ask? With your false story, you   Du fragst? War's nicht dein Zeugniss,
  persuaded   deine Kunde,
me to accuse an innocent of murder?   die mich bestrickt, die Reine zu
    verklagen?
Can you deny you lied to me, telling   Die du im düst'ren Wald zu Haus,
    log'st du
me how, outside your gloomy castle,   mir nicht, von deinem wilden Schlosse
    aus
you saw the crime committed in the   die Unthat habest du verüben seh'n?
  wood?
You said you saw Elsa take her brother   Mit eig'nem Aug', wie Elsa selbst den
    Bruder
and drown him in the lake. You can't   im Weiher dort ertränkt? Umstricktest
  deny   du
that you seduced me with prophecies   mein stolzes Herz durch die Weissagung
  and lies: nicht,
you said the ancient house of Radbod   bald würde Radbod's alter Fürstenstamm
once more would blossom and flourish   von Neuem grünen und herrschen in
  in Brabant.   Brabant?
Did you not thus persuade me to reject   Bewog'st du so mich nicht, von Elsa's
    Hand,
my Elsa, who is good, and take your hand   der reinen, abzusteh'n, und dich zum Weib
in marriage, as you're the last of   zu nehmen, weil du Radbod's letzter
  Radbod's line?   Spross'?

ORTRUD
(quietly, but angrily)

Ah! you wound me to the quick!   Ha, wie tödtlich du mich kränkst!
(aloud)
They're not lies, no, I told the truth to   Diess alles, ja! ich sagt' und zeugt' es dir.
  you!

FREDERICK
(very animatedly)

And you made me, whose name was   Und machtest mich, dess' Name
  well esteemed,   hochgeehrt,
who prized a life of honour above all,   dess' Leben aller höchsten Tugend Preis,
the base accomplice to your shameless   zu deiner Lüge schändlichem Genossen?
  lying!

ORTRUD
(defiantly)

Who lied?   Wer log?

FREDERICK

You! That's why I lost the fight: Du! Hat nicht durch sein Gericht
God punished me for your lies!   Gott mich dafür geschlagen?

ORTRUD
(with terrible scorn)

God?   Gott?

FREDERICK

<table>
<tr><td>You monster!</td><td>Entsetzlich!</td></tr>
<tr><td>How terrible that holy name
  sounds on your lips!</td><td>Wie tönt aus deinem Munde furchtbar
  der Name!</td></tr>
</table>

ORTRUD

Ah! would you call your cowardice God?	Ha, nennst du deine Feigheit Gott?

FREDERICK

<table>
<tr><td>Ortrud!</td><td>Ortrud!</td></tr>
</table>

ORTRUD

You'd threaten me? Threaten a woman? You?	Willst du mir droh'n? Mir, einem Weibe — droh'n?
O coward! If you'd threatened him instead	O Feiger! Hättest du so grimmig ihm
of me, you'd threatened him who caused your shame,	gedroht, der jetzt dich in das Elend schickt,
you would have won the victory yourself!	wohl hättest Sieg statt Schande du erkauft!
Ah! one who was a match for him would find	Ha, wer ihm zu entgegnen wüsst', der fänd'
him weaker than a child!	ihn schwächer als ein Kind!

FREDERICK

If he was weak,	Je schwächer er,
then all the stronger would be God's support!	desto gewalt'ger kämpfte Gottes Kraft.

ORTRUD

God's support? Aha!	Gottes Kraft? Ha! ha!
Give me the chance and I will prove to you	Gieb hier mir Macht, und sicher zeig' ich dir,
how feeble is the God that shelters him.	welch' schwacher Gott es ist, der ihn beschützt.

FREDERICK
(seized by fear, with a hushed and trembling voice)

You crazy sorceress! I fear	Du wilde Seherin! Wie willst du doch
your scheming promises will once again bewitch me!	geheimnissvoll den Geist mir neu berücken?

ORTRUD
(pointing to the banqueting hall, where the lights are now extinguished)

The bloated revellers are fast asleep;	Die Schwelger streckten sich zur üpp'gen Ruh'.
come close and sit by me! The time has come	Setz' dich zur Seite mir: die Stund' ist da,
for my prophetic power to enlighten you.	wo dir mein Seherauge leuchten soll.

(Frederick draws closer and closer to Ortrud, lending an attentive ear to all she says.)

Do you know who he is, this dazzling hero brought here by a swan?	Weisst du, wer dieser Held, den hier ein Schwan gezogen an das Land?

FREDERICK

No!	Nein!

ORTRUD

What would you give to know the answer,	Was gäbst du doch, es zu erfahren,
were I to say, if someone forced him to tell us who he really is,	wenn ich dir sag': ist er gezwungen zu nennen wie sein Nam' und Art,
that magic power would disappear and all his strength would drain away?	all' seine Macht zu Ende ist, die mühvoll ihm ein Zauber leiht?

65

FREDERICK

Ah! That explains his strange
command!

Ha! Dann begriff ich sein Verbot!

ORTRUD

But listen! No one here has the power
to extract the secret from him
save she whom he so strictly forbade
to ever ask his name.

Nun hör'! Niemand hier hat Gewalt
ihm das Geheimniss zu entreissen,
als die, der er so streng verbot
die Frage je an ihn zu thun.

FREDERICK

You mean that Elsa must be tempted
to ask the question he forbids?

So gält' es, Elsa zu verleiten,
dass sie die Frag' ihm nicht erliess'?

ORTRUD

Ah! You have understood me well!

Ha, wie begreifst du schnell und wohl!

FREDERICK

But how can we persuade her?

Doch wie soll das gelingen?

ORTRUD

Think!
Above all else we must not leave
this place; now keep your wits about
you!
We'll start by making her suspicious
(very emphatically)
and then charge him with sorcery,
with which he even cheated God!

Hör'!
Vor allem gilt's, von hinnen nicht
zu flieh'n: drum schärfe deinen Witz!

Gerechten Argwohn ihr zu wecken,

tritt vor, klag ihn des Zaubers an,
mit dem er das Gericht getäuscht!

FREDERICK
(with mounting inner rage)

Ah! Curse his foul deceit!

Ha! Trug und Zauber's List!

ORTRUD

If that fails
then we'll succeed by using force.

Misglückt's,
so bleibt ein Mittel der Gewalt.

FREDERICK

With force?

Gewalt?

ORTRUD
(somewhat more slowly)

It's not in vain that I
am versed in Nature's darkest secrets;
so listen well to what I tell you!
One who possesses magic strength
will, if the smallest of his limbs
is torn from him, at once be seen
stripped of his power, yes, exposed!

Umsonst nicht bin ich in
geheimsten Künsten tief erfahren!
drum achte wohl, was ich dir sage!
Jed' Wesen, das durch Zauber stark,
wird ihm des Leibes kleinstes Glied
entrissen nur, muss sich alsbald
ohnmächtig zeigen, wie es ist.

FREDERICK
(very quickly)

Would this were true!

Ha, spräch'st du wahr!

ORTRUD
(animatedly)

Yes! If you in
the fight had cut his finger off,
even the tip of his little finger,
the victory would have been yours!

O hättest du
im Kampf nur einen Finger ihm,
ja, eines Fingers Glied entschlagen,
der Held, er war in deiner Macht!

FREDERICK

Oh, horror! Ah! I can hardly believe it!

Entsetzlich, ha! Was lässest du mich
hören?

But God, I thought, had conquered me:

(with terrible bitterness)

but now I find this nameless man deceived me,
through magic tricks I was condemned for life!

Can I avenge the shame I suffer
and prove myself the best of men,
reveal the evil of her lover

and find my honour once again?
O woman, here before me in the night,

if you're deceiving me, God strike you dead!

Durch Gott geschlagen wähnt ich mich,

nun liess durch Trug sich das Gericht bethören,
durch Zauber's List verlor mein' Ehre ich!

Doch meine Schande könnt' ich rächen?
Bezeugen könnt' ich meine Treu'?
Des Buhlen Trug, ich könnt' ihn brechen,

und meine Ehr' gewänn' ich neu?
O Weib, das in der Nacht ich vor mir seh'!

Betrügst du jetzt mich noch, dann weh' dir, weh'!

ORTRUD

Ah! Why so angry? Calm yourself! Be patient!
Soon you will know revenge's sweetest moments!

Ha, wie du rasest! Ruhig und besonnen!

So lehr' ich dich der Rache süsse Wonnen.

Frederick slowly sits down at Ortrud's side.

ORTRUD AND FREDERICK

My bitter heart cries out for vengeance,   [16]
it will destroy the foe it hates!
You who are lost in blissful slumber,
soon you shall know disaster waits!

Der Rache Werk sei nun beschworen

aus meines Busens wilder Nacht.
Die ihr in süssem Schlaf verloren,
wisst, dass für euch das Unheil wacht!

A door leading onto the balcony of the women's quarters is opened.

Scene Two. *Dressed all in white, Elsa appears on the balcony; she moves forward to the balustrade and rests her head on her hand; Frederick and Ortrud remain seated on the Minster steps opposite her.* [17]

ELSA

You breezes who so often
have carried my sad songs,
gratefully I shall tell you
to whom my heart belongs.
You smiled down on his journey,
you calmed the stormy sea,
protected him from danger
and brought him here to me.
No longer need you carry
my sighs to Heaven above;
but cool my cheeks I beg you,
my cheeks that burn with love!

Euch Lüften, die mein Klagen,
so traurig oft erfüllt,
euch muss ich dankend sagen,
wie sich mein Glück enthüllt.
Durch euch kam er gezogen,
ihr lächeltet der Fahrt;
auf wilden Meereswogen
habt ihr ihn treu bewahrt.
Zu trock'nen meine Zähren
hab' ich euch oft gemüht:
wollt' Kühlung nun gewähren
der Wang', in Lieb' erglüht!

ORTRUD

She's there!

Sie ist es!

FREDERICK

Elsa!

Elsa.

ORTRUD

Her dreams of joy will vanish
as soon as she sets eyes on me! Away!

Until I call, keep out of sight!

Der Stunde soll sie fluchen,
in der sie jetzt mein Blick gewahrt!
Hinweg!
Entfern' ein Kleines dich von mir!

FREDERICK

Why?   Warum?

ORTRUD

I'll deal with her, and him I leave to you!   Sie ist für mich, — ihr Held gehöre dir!

Frederick withdraws and disappears upstage.
(calling out, with a plaintive expression)

Elsa!   Elsa!

ELSA

Who's that! How mournful and how
plaintive
my name re-echoes through the night!

Wer ruft! Wie schauerlich und
klagend
ertönt mein Name durch die Nacht!

ORTRUD

Elsa!   Elsa!
Do you not recognize my voice?
Have you forgotten and disowned her
whom you condemned to live in
shame?

Ist meine Stimme dir so fremd?
Willst du die Ärmste ganz verläugnen,
die du in's fernste Elend schick'st?

ELSA

Ortrud! It's you? Be gone from here,

ill-fated woman!

Ortrud! Bist du's? Was machst du
hier,
unglücklich Weib?

ORTRUD

'Ill-fated woman' ...   Unglücklich Weib?
Oh, you are right, so to address me!
Alone and hidden in the forest
I lived a quiet peaceful life.
What can it be I've done to you?
Sadly lamenting the misfortune
so long inflicted on my house,
what can it be I've done to you?

Wohl hast du recht mich so zu nennen!
In ferner Einsamkeit des Waldes,
wo still and friedsam ich gelebt,
was that ich dir? Was that ich dir?
Freudlos, das Unglück nur beweinend,
das lang' belastet meinen Stamm
was that ich dir? Was that ich dir?

ELSA

O God, you come to me for help?
Was I the cause of your disgrace?

Um Gott, was klagest du mich an?
War ich es, die dir Leid gebracht?

ORTRUD

How could you envy me my fortune
when I was chosen as the bride

of him whom you so gladly scorned?

Wie könntest du fürwahr mir neiden
das Glück, dass mich zum Weib
erwählt
der Mann, den du so gern verschmäht?

ELSA

O God in Heaven! What can you
mean!

Allgüt'ger Gott, was soll mir das?

ORTRUD

He must have been possessed by
madness
to charge you with that dreadful crime.
Now stricken with remorse and
sadness,
to grim repentance he's confined.

Musst' ihn unsel'ger Wahn bethören,

dich Reine einer Schuld zu zeih'n,
von Reu' ist nun sein Herz zerrissen,

zu grimmer Buss' ist er verdammt.

ELSA

Almighty God!   Gerechter Gott!

ORTRUD

Oh, you are happy!   O du bist glücklich!
Your fleeting sorrows all are over,   Nach kurzem, unschuldsüssem Leiden

68

life laughs and smiles with honeyed
    breath;
you'll gladly turn away and shun me,
you'll send me on the road to death,
so that my misery and pain
will never trouble you again!

siehst lächeln du das Leben nur;

von mir darfst selig du dich scheiden,
mich schickst du auf des Todes Spur,
dass meines Jammer's trüber Schein
nie kehr' in deine Feste ein.

ELSA
(deeply moved)

I know that I would seem ungrateful,
o generous God in whom I trust,
were I to cast aside the suppliant
that lies before me in the dust!
Oh, never, Ortrud! Speak no more!
Wait there, I shall unlock the door.

Wie schlecht ich deine Güte priese,
Allmächt'ger, der mich so beglückt,
wenn ich das Unglück von mir stiesse,
das sich im Staube vor mir bückt!
O nimmer! - Ortrud! Harre mein!
Ich selber lass' dich zu mir ein.

She hurries back into the women's quarters. Ortrud leaps up from the steps in wild enthusiasm.

ORTRUD

Eternal spirits! Guide me to my
    vengeance!
Avenge our shame, dishonour and
    disgrace!
Help me to shatter their vile delusions

and tear her away from his foul embrace!

Wotan! I beg you strengthen me!
Freia! I beg you smile on me!
Bless the deceit of my design,
that vengeance may at last be mine!

Entweihte Götter! Helft jetzt meiner
    Rache!
Bestraft die Schmach, die hier euch
    angethan!
Stärkt mich im Dienst eurer heil'gen
    Sache,
vernichtet der Abtrünn'gen schnöden
    Wahn!

Wodan! Dich Starken rufe ich!
Freia! Erhab'ne, höre mich!
Segnet mir Trug und Heuchelei,
dass glücklich meine Rache sei!

ELSA
(still outside)

Ortrud! Where are you!

Ortrud! Wo bist du?

Elsa and two maidservants with lights enter by the lower door.

ORTRUD
(humbly throwing herself at Elsa's feet)

Here I fall before you!

Hier, zu deinen Füssen!

ELSA
(starting back in alarm on seeing Ortrud)

Dear God! What do I see before me?
You were so proud and grand of late!
It fills my heart with grief and pity,
seeing you reduced to such a state!
Stand up! Oh, spare your supplication!
Even your hate I shall forgive.
If I have caused you pain and sorrow,
I beg of you, forgive me too!

Hilf Gott! So muss ich dich erblicken,
die ich in Stolz und Pracht nur sah!
Es will das Herze mir ersticken,
seh' ich so niedrig dich mir nah'.
Steh' auf! O spare mir dein Bitten!
Trug'st du mir Hass, verzieh ich dir;
Was du schon jetzt durch mich gelitten,
das, bitte ich, verzeih' auch mir!

ORTRUD

O let me thank you for your kindness!

O habe Dank für so viel Güte!

ELSA

Tomorrow I shall be a bride,
then I shall ask my sweet-natured
    husband
if Frederick may now be reprieved.

Der morgen nun mein Gatte heisst,
an fleh' ich sein liebreich Gemüthe,

dass Friedrich auch er Gnad' erweist.

ORTRUD

I shall be in your debt for ever!

Du fesselst mich in Dankes Banden!

ELSA
(with increasingly rapt excitement)

At dawn it's you I want to see;	In Früh'n lass mich bereit dich seh'n!
attired in splendid festive garments,	Geschmückt mit prächtigen Gewanden,
then to the minster come with me.	sollst du mit mir zum Münster geh'n:
All that I have is his for life:	dort harre ich des Helden mein,

(with joyful pride and, finally, blissful rapture)

there God will make us man and wife!	vor Gott sein Eh'gemahl zu sein.

ORTRUD

How can I find a way to thank you,	Wie kann ich solche Huld dir lohnen,
forlorn and wretched as I am?	da machtlos ich und elend bin?
Were I to spend my life beside you,	Soll ich in Gnaden bei dir wohnen,
I'd always be the servile one.	stets bleibe ich die Bettlerin.

(gradually approaching Elsa)

One single power remains within me,	Nur eine Macht ist mir geblieben,
no one can take this one away;	sie raubte mir kein Machtgebot;
with it perhaps I could protect you	durch sie vielleicht schütz' ich dein Leben,
and save you from remorse one day.	bewahr' es vor der Reue Noth.

ELSA
(in an artless, friendly manner)

Protect me?	Wie meinst du?

ORTRUD
(forcefully)

Listen to my warning!	Wohl dass ich dich warne,

(moderating her tone)

Beware your carefree trust in fate!	zu blind nicht deinem Glück zu trau'n;
I see disaster in your future.	dass nicht ein Unheil dich umgarne,
Listen before it is too late!	lass mich für dich zur Zukunft schau'n.

ELSA
(with secret dread)

Disaster?	Welch' Unheil?

ORTRUD
(very mysteriously)

Don't let him deceive you,	Könntest du erfassen,
that man for whom you have no name!	wie dessen Art so wundersam,
Can you be sure he'll never leave you	der nie dich möge so verlassen,
and disappear the way he came?	wie er durch Zauber zu dir kam!

Seized by dread, Elsa turns away in her anger but then turns back to Ortrud, full of sadness and pity.

ELSA
(somewhat freely declaimed)

Poor Ortrud, you cannot imagine	Du Ärmste kannst wohl nie ermessen,
how free of needless doubts I live!	wie zweifellos mein Herze liebt!
Maybe you've never known the pleasure	Das hast wohl nie das Glück besessen,
that only faith and love can give.	das sich uns nur durch Glauben giebt!
Come to my side! Ah, let me teach you	Kehr' bei mir ein, lass mich dich lehren
the joy of trust that knows no threat.	wie süss die Wonne reinster Treu'!
Try to believe me, I beseech you:	Lass zu dem Glauben dich bekehren:
there can be joy without regret!	Es giebt ein Glück, das ohne Reu'.

ORTRUD
(aside)

Ah, foolish girl, now I shall teach you,	Ha! Dieser Stolz, er soll mich lehren,
your simple trust will catch you yet!	wie ich bekämpfe ihre Treu':
I know the perfect way to reach you,	gen ihn will ich die Waffen kehren,
and that proud heart will feel regret!	durch ihren Hochmuth werd' ihr Reu'!

Accompanied by Elsa, Ortrud goes through the small door with hypocritical hesitation; the maidservants light their way, closing the door behind them. First signs of dawn. Frederick emerges from the shadows.

FREDERICK

So evil moves into this house!
The die is cast: your plan must be completed.
I have no strength to stop what you've begun.
And Elsa, by whose hand I was defeated,

now she shall fall and justice will be done!
One single thought remains my constant cry:
the man who took my honour, he must die!

So zieht das Unheil in dies Haus!
Vollführe, Weib, was deine List ersonnen;
dein Werk zu hemmen fühl' ich keine Macht.
Das Unheil hat mit meinem Fall begonnen,

nun stürzet nach, die mich dahin gebracht!
Nur eines seh' ich mahnend vor mir steh'n:
der Räuber meiner Ehre soll vergeh'n!

Frederick looks for the best place to hide from the thronging crowd, then conceals himself behind a protruding section of the minster wall.

Scene Three. *Day gradually breaks over the scene. Two watchmen sound the reveille from the tower; it is answered from a distant tower. When the watchmen descend from their tower and open the gate, servants arrive from various directions, greet each other and quietly set about their various duties: some draw water from the well in metal containers and knock at the door of the banqueting hall, to which they are duly admitted. The banqueting-hall door is again opened, the King's four trumpeters emerge and sound the summons. They then return to the banqueting hall. By now the servants, too, have left the stage. Nobles and inhabitants of the castle now enter in ever-increasing numbers, some from the direction of the town, others from various parts of the castle.*

NOBLES AND VASSALS

The trumpet summons us at dawn, [18]
the day with expectation rings.
The man who has done miracles
today may do more wondrous things.

In Frühn versammelt uns der Ruf:
gar viel verheisset wohl der Tag.
Der hier so hehre Wunder schuf,
manch' neue That vollbringen mag.

The Herald comes out of the banqueting hall, preceded by the four trumpeters. All turn upstage in great expectation.

HERALD
(on an elevation outside the entrance to the banqueting hall)

I bring you the command of the king;

so listen well to what I have to say!

Frederick Telramund is banished
because he dared to challenge even God.
According to the law of the land,

the man who shelters him shall himself be banned.

Des Königs Wort und Will' thu' ich euch kund:

drum achtet wohl, was euch durch mich er sagt!

In Bann und Acht ist Friedrich Telramund,
weil untreu er den Gotteskampf gewagt:
wer sein noch pflegt, wer sich zu ihm gesellt,

nach Reiches Recht derselben Acht verfällt.

MEN

Curse him, for he is shameless,
he has offended God!
Shunned by the pure and blameless,
may he not sleep nor rest!

Fluch ihm, dem Ungetreuen,
den Gottes Urtheil traf!
Ihn soll der Reine scheuen,
es flieh' ihn Ruh' und Schlaf!

At the sound of the trumpets, the townspeople quickly resume their former attentive attitude.

HERALD

And furthermore the king has proclaimed
that the stranger sent to us by God,

the man who has accepted Elsa's hand,

Und weiter kündet euch der König an,
dass er den fremden gottgesandten Mann,

den Elsa zum Gemahle sich ersehnt,

71

shall be your leader and shall rule this land.	mit Land und Krone von Brabant belehnt.
But since he has declined the name of Duke,	Doch will der Held nicht Herzog sein genannt,
he shall be called Protector of Brabant!	ihr sollt ihn heissen: Schützer von Brabant!

MEN

Yes, he will defend our land!	Hoch der ersehnte Mann!
The man whom God has sent!	Heil ihm, den Gott gesandt!
We shall be true to the Protector of Brabant.	Treu sind wir unterthan dem Schützer von Brabant.

HERALD

And now the great Protector bids me say:	Nun hört, was er durch mich euch sagen lässt!
you are invited to his wedding day.	Heut' feiert er mit euch sein Hochzeitsfest:
Tomorrow then be ready, swords in hand,	doch morgen sollt ihr kampfgerüstet nah'n,
to serve the king as soldiers of this land.	zur Heeresfolg' dem König unterthan.
He shall forgo all further celebration	Er selbst verschmäht der süssen Ruh' zu pflegen,
and lead to victory this glorious nation!	er führt euch an zu hehren Ruhmes Segen!

The Herald shortly returns to the banqueting hall, together with the four trumpeters.

MEN
(enthusiastically)

We'll go without delay!		Zum Streite säumet nicht,
The hero leads us on!		führt euch der Hehre an!
We'll boldly join the fray!	[19]	Wer muthig mit ihm ficht,
On us his light has shone!		dem lacht des Ruhmes Bahn.
From God he has been sent,		Von Gott ist er gesandt
the saviour of Brabant!		zur Grösse von Brabant!

While the crowd surges joyfully to and fro, four Nobles — Frederick's former liegemen — move to the front of the stage.

THIRD NOBLE

You heard? He means to lead us into danger!	Nun hört! Dem Lande will er uns entführen?

SECOND NOBLE

Against a foe we have no cause to hate.	Gen einen Feind, der uns noch nie bedroht?

FOURTH NOBLE

His rash decision cannot be accepted!	Solch' kühn Beginnen sollt' ihm nicht gebühren!

FIRST NOBLE

Who'll stop him though? Now it is much too late!	Wer wehret ihm, wenn er die Fahrt gebot?

Frederick has joined them unnoticed.

FREDERICK

No!	Ich.

He uncovers his head. They start back, horrified.

THE FOUR NOBLES

Ah! Who are you? Frederick! What a risk!	Ha! Wer bist du? - Friedrich! Seh' ich recht!
You dare to risk the price upon your head?	Du wagst dich her, zur Beute jedem Knecht?

72

The risk I'm here to take is even greater:	Gar bald will ich wohl weiter noch mich wagen!
before your eyes I shall reveal the traitor!	Vor euren Augen soll es leuchtend tagen!
The man who proudly leads you off to war,	Der euch so kühn die Heerfahrt angesagt,
he is not sent by God, of that I'm sure!	der sei von mir des Gottestrug's beklagt!

THE FOUR NOBLES

You're crazy! Madman! You must be mad!	Was hör' ich? Rasender, was hast du vor?
Beware! Be careful or they will hear!	Verlor'ner du, hört dich des Volkes Ohr!

Four pages come out onto the terrace in front of the women's quarters, then run merrily over to the raised ground outside the entrance to the banqueting hall, where they take up their positions. The nobles force Frederick towards the Minster, trying to conceal him from the gaze of the townspeople. On seeing the pages, the townspeople crowd to the front of the stage.

THE FOUR PAGES
(on the raised ground in front of the banqueting hall)

Make way! Our lady Elsa's here!	Macht Platz für Elsa, unsre Frau!
She will be married here today!	Die will in Gott zum Münster geh'n.

They move downstage, opening up a wide passage between the rows of nobles, who willingly fall back before them, before taking up their new positions on the Minster steps. Four more pages enter from the women's quarters with measured and solemn tread and take up their positions on the terrace in readiness to escort the expected train of women.

Scene Four. *A long train of women, magnificently attired, slowly emerges onto the terrace through the door of the women's quarters, then moves to the left, past the banqueting hall, from where they turn back downstage towards the Minster, on the steps of which the first to arrive take up their positions. Elsa comes into view as part of the procession. The nobles deferentially bare their heads.* [20]

NOBLES AND VASSALS

May Heaven's blessing guide her	Gesegnet soll sie schreiten,
who suffered in despair;	die lang in Demuth litt!
may God remain beside her	Gott möge sie geleiten,
and keep her in His care.	Gott hüte ihren Schritt!

(The nobles have involuntarily pressed forward but once again fall back before the pages, who make way for the procession, which is now already outside the banqueting hall. By this point Elsa has reached the raised ground outside the banqueting hall: the passage is open once again, so that everyone can see Elsa, who remains standing here for a moment.)

She's here! How like an angel	Sie naht, die Engelgleiche,
she glows so fair and chaste!	von keuscher Gluth entbrannt!

(Elsa slowly moves downstage between the rows of men.)

Bless you, o virtuous lady!	Heil dir, o Tugendreiche!

(By now, not only the pages but the leading women have reached the steps of the Minster, where they take up their positions in order to allow Elsa to enter the church before them.)

Hail, Elsa of Brabant!	Heil Elsa von Brabant!

As Elsa places her foot on the second step of the Minster, Ortrud — who has hitherto been at the back of the procession — rushes forward and places herself on the same step, thus confronting Elsa directly.

ORTRUD

Go back, Elsa! I can no longer bear it	Zurück, Elsa! Nicht länger will ich dulden,
to follow like a servant after you!	dass ich gleich einer Magd dir folgen soll!
To me you must give precedence in future,	Den Vortritt sollst du überall mir schulden,
you'll have to bow and show me due respect!	vor mir dich beugen sollst du demuthvoll!

What does she want?   Was will das Weib?

ELSA
(violently startled)

O God! What does she mean?   Um Gott! Was muss ich seh'n?
What sudden change has overtaken you?   Welch' jäher Wechsel ist mit dir
                                             gescheh'n?

ORTRUD

Since for one hour my self-esteem departed,   Weil eine Stund' ich meines Werth's
                                          vergessen,
you assume, before you I must crawl and quake!   glaubest du, ich müsste dir nur kriechend
                                          nah'n?
I shall have vengeance for the wrongs I suffered;   Mein Leid zu rächen will ich mich
                                          vermessen,
what's mine by right, that I intend to take.   was mir gebührt, das will ich nun empfah'n.

Lively astonishment and agitation.

ELSA

Ah! It was your hypocrisy that deceived me!   Weh'! Liess ich durch dein Heucheln
                                          mich verleiten,
Only last night my sympathy you claimed.   die diese Nacht sich jammernd zu mir
                                          stahl?
How can you think that you should now precede me?   Wie willst du nun in Hochmuth vor mir
                                          schreiten,
You, wife of one whom God condemned and shamed!   du, eines Gottgerichteten Gemahl?

ORTRUD
(proudly, but appearing to be deeply hurt)

When he was falsely condemned and banished,   Wenn falsch Gericht mir den Gemahl
                                          verbannte,
his worthy name was honoured and revered.   war doch sein Nam' im Lande hochgeehrt;
All knew him as a man of noble virtue,   als aller Tugend Preis man ihn nur
                                          nannte,
in times of war his mighty sword was feared.   gekannt, gefürchtet war sein tapf'res
                                          Schwert.
But your man, well, nothing is known about him;   Der deine, sag', wer sollte hier ihn
                                          kennen,
you have yourself no name by which to call him!   vermagst du selbst den Namen nicht zu
                                          nennen?

MEN AND WOMEN

What is this? Ah! How can she dare?   Was sagt sie? Ha! Was thut sie kund?
Blasphemer! She must be restrained!   Sie lästert! Wehret ihrem Mund!

ORTRUD
(not too slowly)

So can you name him? Can you prove he's noble?   Kannst du ihn nennen? Kannst du uns
                                          es sagen,
Why don't you tell us everything you know?   ob sein Geschlecht, sein Adel wohl
                                          bewährt?
Where did he come from, riding on the water?   Woher die Fluthen ihn zu dir getragen,
When will he leave and where will he then go?   wann und wohin er wieder von dir fährt?
Ah no! Since it would bring about his fall,   Ha, nein! Wohl brächte ihm es schlimme
                                          Noth;
she's not allowed to question him at all!   der kluge Held die Frage drob verbot!

Ah! Is this the truth? What dreadful charges!	Ha, spricht sie wahr? Welch' schwere Klagen!
She slanders him! How can she dare to?	Sie schmähet ihn! Darf sie es wagen?

ELSA
(recovering from her great astonishment)

You slanderer! You evil witch!	Du Lästerin! Ruchlose Frau!
This is the answer I shall give!	Hör', ob ich Antwort mir getrau'!

(with great warmth)

The man who saved me is so noble,	So rein und edel ist sein Wesen,
so pure and good, so filled with love,	so tugendreich der hehre Mann,
the one who doubts his virtuous calling	dass nie des Unheil's soll genesen,
shall be condemned by God above!	wer seiner Sendung zweifeln kann!

MEN

Oh, yes!	Gewiss!

ELSA

You saw yourself who lost the combat	Hat nicht durch Gott im Kampf geschlagen
and was condemned by God to shame!	mein theurer Held den Gatten dein?

(to the townspeople)

Now let the people give their answer:	Nun sollt nach Recht ihr alle sagen,
which of the two is not to blame?	wer kann da nur der Reine sein?

MEN AND WOMEN

She's right! She's right! Elsa is right!	Nur er! Nur er! Dein Held allein!

ORTRUD
(mocking Elsa)

Ah! So he's perfect, your great hero!	Ha! Diese Reine deines Helden,
How soon his dazzling strength would fade	wie wäre sie so bald getrübt,
if he were forced by her to tell us	müsst' er des Zaubers Wesen melden,
by what magical power it's made!	durch den hier solche Macht er übt!
And if you never dare to ask him,	Wagst du ihn nicht darum zu fragen,

(very emphatically)

we all will rightfully believe	so glauben alle wir mit Recht,
that you yourself have doubts about him	du müssest selbst in Sorge zagen,
because you fear you are deceived!	um seine Reine steh' es schlecht!

The doors of the banqueting hall are opened and the King's four trumpeters come out and sound their call.

WOMEN
(supporting Elsa)

Shield her from this woman's hate!	Helft ihr vor der Verruchten Hass!

MEN
(looking upstage)

Make way! Make way! The King is here!	Macht Platz! Macht Platz! Der König naht!

Scene Five. *The King, Lohengrin and the Saxon counts and nobles have emerged from the banqueting hall in a solemn procession, but their progress is interrupted by the disturbance at the front of the stage. The King and Lohengrin move quickly downstage.*

MEN

Hail! Hail Your Highness!	Heil! Heil dem König!
Hail! Protector of Brabant!	Heil dem Schützer von Brabant!

KING HENRY

What's happened here? | Was für ein Streit?

ELSA
(throwing herself on Lohengrin's breast in her agitation)

My lord! Help me, protect me! | Mein Herr! O mein Gebieter!

LOHENGRIN

What's wrong? | Was ist?

KING HENRY

Who dares to block our way to the cathedral? | Wer wagt es hier, den Kirchengang zu stören?

THE KING'S RETINUE

It is her! She's causing trouble! | Welcher Streit, den wir vernahmen?

LOHENGRIN
(catching sight of Ortrud)

That heathen! Why's that woman here with you? | Was seh' ich? Das unsel'ge Weib bei dir?

ELSA

My Saviour! Stand by me against this witch! | Mein Retter! Schütze mich vor dieser Frau!
Scold me, if I have disobeyed your will! | Schilt mich, wenn ich dir ungehorsam war!
I found her desperate outside the castle; I couldn't bear to see her in such pain: now look how cruelly she repays my kindness — | In Jammer sah ich sie vor dieser Pforte, aus ihrer Noth nahm ich sie bei mir auf: nun sieh', wie furchtbar sie mir lohnt die Güte,
she tells me I am wrong to trust in you! | sie schilt mich, dass ich dir zu sehr vertrau'!

LOHENGRIN
(fixing his eyes commandingly on Ortrud, who is incapable of moving)

You dark and fearsome woman! Away from her! | Du fürchterliches Weib! Steh' ab von ihr!
Here you will never win! | Hier wird dir nimmer Sieg!
(He turns gently to Elsa.)
Elsa, I hope you have not let her fill your heart with poison. | Sag', Elsa, mir! Vermocht' ihr Gift sie in dein Herz zu giessen?
(Weeping, Elsa hides her face on his breast.)
Come! It is time to shed tears of joy, not sorrow! | Komm'! Lass in Freude dort diese Thränen fliessen!

Lohengrin raises her up and points to the Minster. Together with Elsa and the King, he turns to lead the procession to the Minster; all prepare to follow in due order. Frederick suddenly appears on the Minster steps; the women and pages start back in horror.

FREDERICK

Oh! Listen! He is an imposter! Hear me out! | O König! Trugbethörte Fürsten! Haltet ein!

ALL THE MEN

What does he want? Blasphemer! Go, you're banished! | Was will der hier? Verfluchter, weich' von dannen!

FREDERICK

Listen to me! | O hört mich an!

KING HENRY

Get out! Go! You are banished! | Zurück! Weiche von dannen!

Away! Or you will soon be dead!　　　　Hinweg! Du bist des Todes, Mann!

FREDERICK

Listen! The way you treated me was　　Hört mich, dem grimmes Unrecht ihr
wrong!　　　　　　　　　　　　　　gethan!
God's holy will has been defiled and　　Gottes Gericht, es ward entehrt, betrogen,
cheated!
By tricks and sorcery I was defeated!　　durch eines Zaubrer's List seid ihr
　　　　　　　　　　　　　　　　　belogen!

KING HENRY AND THE MEN

Seize the blasphemer! Ah! He must be　　Greift den Verruchten! Hört, er lästert
mad!　　　　　　　　　　　　　　　Gott!

They close in on him from all sides.

FREDERICK
(with the most frenzied effort to be heard, he fixes his eyes on Lohengrin alone and pays no heed to his assailants)

Your glorious knight, I now accuse　　　Den dort im Glanz ich vor mir sehe,
him,
your hero with his mighty sword!　　　den klage ich des Zauber's an!
(His assailants recoil and finally listen attentively.)
His strength is only an illusion,　　　　Wie Staub vor Gottes Hauch verwehe
a power that he obtained by fraud!　　　die Macht, die er durch List gewann!
What fools you were to watch in　　　　Wie schlecht ihr des Gerichtes wahrtet,
silence
as I was robbed of my good name;　　　das doch die Ehre mir benahm,
if you had asked one simple question,　　da eine Frag' ihr ihm erspartet,
he would have turned and fled in　　　als er zum Gotteskampfe kam!
shame!
No longer can you prevent that　　　　Die Frage nun sollt ihr nicht wehren,
question,
for I shall ask it now myself!　　　　　dass sie ihm jetzt von mir gestellt:
(adopting a commanding attitude)
Who are you? Where have you come　　nach Namen, Stand und Ehren
from?
I ask out loud for all to hear!　　　　frag' ich ihn laut vor aller Welt.
(General movement of consternation.)
Who is he who arrived by magic　　　Wer ist er, der an's Land
　　　　　　　　　　　　　　　　　geschwommen,
in a boat drawn by a wild swan?　　　gezogen von einem wilden Schwan?
If he can conjure swans to help him,　　Wem solche Zauberthiere frommen,
your trust in him is clearly wrong!　　　dess' Reinheit achte ich für Wahn.
Now I insist he answers me;　　　　　Nun soll der Klag' er Rede steh'n:
(animatedly)
if he does so, I'll admit defeat.　　　vermag er's, so geschah mir Recht,
If not, then everyone will see　　　　wo nicht, so sollet ihr ersch'n,
that all his virtue is deceit!　　　　　um seine Reine steh' es schlecht!

All gaze at Lohengrin, dismayed and expectant.

KING HENRY AND THE MEN

What serious charges! Will he agree to　　Welch' harte Klagen! Was wird er ihm
answer?　　　　　　　　　　　　　entgegnen?

LOHENGRIN

I need not justify my presence　　　　Nicht dir, der so vergass der Ehren,
to you whose heart is black with sin!　　hab' Noth ich Rede hier zu steh'n!
The doubts of evil men won't touch　　Des Bösen Zweifel darf ich wehren,
me:
to them I never will give in!　　　　vor ihm wird Reine nie vergeh'n.

FREDERICK

Since he considers me unworthy,
you, Sire, must question him again.
Would he deny your right to ask him?
Could he refuse to answer then?

Darf ich ihm nicht als würdig gelten,
dich ruf' ich, König hochgeehrt!
Wird er auch dich unadlig schelten,
dass er die Frage dir verwehrt?

LOHENGRIN

Yes, I'd refuse even His Highness
and all the princes of this earth!
They have no cause to doubt my
virtue,
they saw and recognized my worth!
There's only one, yes, one to whom I'd
answer:
Elsa —

Ja, selbst dem König darf ich wehren,
und aller Fürsten höchstem Rath!
Nicht darf sie Zweifels Last beschweren,
sie sahen meine gute That.
Nur Eine ist's, — der muss ich Antwort
geben:
Elsa —

(Lohengrin stops in consternation when, turning towards Elsa, he sees her staring ahead of her, her breast heaving violently in wild inner conflict.)

Elsa! She looks so pale and
frightened!
Their evil poison has begun to change
her,
she has been poisoned by the hate
they've shown!
O Heaven! Shelter her from this great
danger
or doubt may enter Elsa's virtuous soul!

Elsa! Wie seh' ich sie erbeben!
In wildem Brüten muss ich sie
gewahren!
Hat sie bethört des Hasses Lügenmund?

O Himmel! Schirme sie vor den Gefahren!

Nie werde Zweifel dieser Reinen kund!

FREDERICK AND ORTRUD

The bitter poison has begun to change
her,
the seeds of doubt within her heart are
sown.
Now we will vanquish this mysterious
stranger:
he will be lost, lost if his name is known!

In wildem Brüten darf ich sie gewahren,

der Zweifel keimt in ihres Herzens
Grund;
der mir zur Noth in dieses Land gefahren,

er ist besiegt, wird ihm die Frage kund!

KING HENRY AND ALL THE MEN, WOMEN AND PAGES

What is the secret guarded by the
stranger?
If he'd be lost, the truth must not be
known!
We will protect this hero from all
danger,
since by his deed his noble rank was
shown.

Welch' ein Geheimniss muss der Held
bewahren?
Bringt es ihm Noth, so wahr' es treu
sein Mund!
Wir schirmen ihn, den Edlen, vor
Gefahren;
durch seine That ward uns sein Adel
kund.

ELSA
(staring straight ahead, oblivious to her surroundings)

If he explains, I know he'll be in danger,

before the world he will be all alone.

But he has saved me. How could I betray
him
by asking him to make his secret known?

Ah, if I knew, I'd never tell a stranger,

yet in my heart the seeds of doubt are
sown!

Was er verbirgt, wohl bräct' es ihm
Gefahren,
vor aller Welt spräch' es hier aus sein
Mund:
die er errettet, weh' mir Undankbaren!

verrieth' ich ihn, dass hier es werde
kund.
Wüsst' ich sein Loos, ich wollt' es treu
bewahren;
im Zweifel doch erbebt des Herzens
Grund!

KING HENRY

My friend, ignore his threats and
accusations!

Mein Held! Entgegne kühn dem
Ungetreuen!

You have our trust and need not fear his questions!	Du bist zu hehr, um, was er klagt, zu scheuen!

THE SAXON AND BRABANTINE NOBLES
(crowding round Lohengrin)

We stand by you and never will regret it,	Wir steh'n zu dir, es soll uns nicht gereuen,
for we have recognized your noble worth.	dass wir der Helden Preis in dir erkannt.
Give us your hand! We never will forsake you	Reich' uns die Hand; wir glauben dir in Treuen,
although your name remains to us unknown.	dass hehr dein Nam', auch wenn er nicht genannt.

The men form a circle round Lohengrin, each of them grasping his hand in turn.

LOHENGRIN

You never will regret that you stood by me,	Euch Helden soll der Glaube nicht gereuen,
though both my rank and name remain unknown.	werd' euch mein Nam' und Art auch nie genannt!

Frederick presses close to Elsa, who is still standing alone downstage, brooding to herself.

FREDERICK
(in a low voice, interposing vehemently)

Have faith in me! I can extract his secret, then you will know the truth!	Vertraue mir! Lass dir ein Mittel heissen, das dir Gewissheit schafft.

ELSA
(startled, but in a low voice)

Away from me!	Hinweg von mir!

FREDERICK

Let me cut off the tip of his finger,	Lass mich das kleinste Glied ihm nur entreissen,
his little finger, and I swear to you that will reveal the secret that he hides:	des Fingers Spitze, und ich schwöre dir, was er dir hehlt, sollst frei du vor dir seh'n,
then he'll have to stay and never leave your side!	dir treu, soll nie er dir von hinnen geh'n.

ELSA

He'll never leave!	Ha, nimmermehr!

FREDERICK

I will be near tonight: call me, the deed can easily be done!	Ich bin dir nah' zur Nacht, ruf'st du, ohn' Schaden ist es schnell vollbracht.

LOHENGRIN
(moving quickly downstage)

Elsa, how dare he talk to you!	Elsa, mit wem verkehrst du da?

(in a terrible voice to Ortrud and Frederick)

Away from her, you demons! And never let me see either of you again!	Zurück von ihr, Verfluchte! Dass nie mein Auge je euch wieder bei ihr seh'!

Frederick makes a gesture of the most anguished rage. Lohengrin turns to Elsa, who, at the first sound of his voice, had sunk at his feet as if annihilated.

Elsa, look at me! You must have faith; in you alone rests all our hope of joy.	Elsa, erhebe dich! In deiner Hand, in deiner Treu' liegt alles Glückes Pfand.
Do you have doubts within your heart?	Lässt nicht des Zweifels Macht dich ruh'n?
Do you want to question me?	Willst du die Frage an mich thun?

ELSA

(in the most violent inner agitation and confusion of shame)

My saviour, you have brought me joy.	Mein Retter, der mir Heil gebracht!
I shall be faithful and true.	Mein Held, in dem ich muss vergeh'n!

(emphatically and resolutely)

Far greater than the power of doubt	Hoch über alles Zweifels Macht
shall be my love for you!	soll meine Liebe steh'n!

She sinks upon his breast.

LOHENGRIN

Elsa, bless you! Now we'll be man and wife!	Heil dir, Elsa! Nun lass vor Gott uns geh'n!

Lohengrin solemnly leads Elsa past the nobles to the King. As they pass, the men fall back deferentially.

MEN

Yes, he has been sent from God!	Seht! Er ist von Gott gesandt!
Bless you! Bless Elsa of Brabant!	Heil euch! Heil Elsa von Brabant!
May Heaven's blessing guide you!	Gesegnet sollst du schreiten!
May God remain beside you!	Gott möge dich geleiten!

Led by the King, Lohengrin and Elsa walk slowly towards the Minster.

WOMEN AND PAGES

Bless you, virtuous lady!	Heil dir, Tugendreiche!
Hail Elsa of Brabant!	Heil Elsa von Brabant!

The King and bridal couple have now reached the topmost step of the Minster; Elsa turns to Lohengrin in deep emotion and the latter takes her in his arms. Held in his embrace, she look down from the steps to her right and, with frightened concern, sees Ortrud raising her arm towards her, as though certain of victory; Elsa averts her face in terror. With the King leading the way, Elsa and Lohengrin set off once more to the entrance of the Minster, as the curtain falls.

Wagner's sketch for Act Three, scene one, in the 1850 Weimar production

Act Three

Prelude [21, 22, 23]

Scene One. *The curtain opens. The bridal chamber, with an oriel tower to the right, the window of which is open. Music off-stage; the singing is heard first in the distance, then closer. In the middle of the singing, doors are opened upstage right and left: the womenfolk enter from the right, accompanying Elsa, while the menfolk, together with the King, enter from the left, accompanying Lohengrin; pages with torches lead the way.*

BRIDAL CHORUS

Husband and wife, enter within, [24]	Treulich geführt ziehet dahin,
brought here together by God's holy grace!	wo euch in Frieden die Liebe bewahr'!
And in this life may you remain	Siegreicher Muth, Minnegewinn
ever united in love's sweet embrace.	eint euch in Treue zum seligsten Paar.
Champion of honour, proudly proceed!	Streiter der Tugend, schreite voran!
Goddess of virtue, proudly proceed!	Zierde der Jugend, schreite voran!
Now that the wedding feasting has ended,	Rauschen des Festes seid nun entronnen,
yours is the silent night that's descended.	Wonne des Herzens sei euch gewonnen!

(At this point the doors are thrown open.)

This fragrant room, prepared for delight,	Duftender Raum, zur Liebe geschmückt,
softly shall hide you both from our sight.	nehm' euch nun auf, dem Glanze entrückt.
Husband and wife, enter within,	Treulich geführt ziehet nun ein,
brought here together by God's holy grace!	wo euch in Segen die Liebe bewahr'!
And in this life may you remain	Siegreicher Muth, Minne so rein
ever united in love's sweet embrace.	eint euch in Treue zum seligsten Paar.

As the two processions meet centre-stage, the women lead Elsa over to Lohengrin; they embrace and remain where they are standing. Eight women walk in solemn procession around Lohengrin and Elsa, whom pages divest of their heavy outer garments.

EIGHT WOMEN
(after circling the couple)

As God has sent his blessing,	Wie Gott euch selig weihte,
we wish you lasting peace;	zu Freuden weih'n euch wir;

(They walk round the couple a second time.)

and from this treasured moment	in Liebesglück's Geleite
may all your joys increase!	denkt lang' der Stunde hier!

The King embraces Lohengrin and Elsa and gives them his blessing. The pages give a signal to withdraw; the processions reform and, during the following, pass in front of the newly-wed couple, so that the menfolk leave the bridal chamber by the right-hand door, the womenfolk by the left-hand door.

BRIDAL CHORUS

Husband and wife, welcome within,	Treulich bewacht bleibet zurück,
brought here together by God's holy grace!	wo euch in Segen die Liebe bewahr'!
And in this life may you remain	Siegreicher Muth, Minne und Glück
ever united in love's sweet embrace.	eint euch in Treue zum seligsten Paar.
Champion of honour, stay by her side!	Streiter der Tugend, bleibe daheim!
Goddess of virtue, stay by his side!	Zierde der Jugend, bleibe daheim!
Now that the wedding feasting has ended,	Rauschen des Festes seid nun entronnen,
yours is the silent night that's descended!	Wonne des Herzens sei euch gewonnen!
This fragrant room, prepared for delight,	Duftender Raum, zur Liebe geschmückt,
softly shall hide you both from our sight.	nahm euch nun auf, dem Glanze entrückt.

(By now the two processions have left the stage, and the doors are closed by the last pair of pages.)
(gradually receding)

Husband and wife, welcome within, brought here together by God's holy grace!	Treulich bewacht bleibet zurück, wo euch in Segen die Liebe bewahr'!
And in this life may you remain	Siegreicher Muth, Minne und Glück

(dying away completely)

ever united in love's sweet embrace.	eint euch in Treue zum seligsten Paar.

As the two processions left the chamber, Elsa had sunk down on Lohengrin's breast in an excess of joy. As the singing dies away, Lohengrin sits on a couch by the oriel window and gently draws Elsa to him.

Scene Two.

LOHENGRIN

The song has died away: we are alone as we have never been since first we met. Now we can both escape the restless world, and every thought that's not of love forget. Elsa, my wife! My sweet and virtuous bride! Oh say you're glad that you are by my side?	Das süsse Lied verhallt; wir sind allein, zum ersten Mal allein, seit wir uns sah'n; nun sollen wir der Welt entronnen sein, kein Lauscher darf des Herzens Grüssen nah'n. Elsa, mein Weib! Du süsse, reine Braut! Ob glücklich du, das sei mir jetzt vertraut!

ELSA

How could I say that I was merely happy when all the joy of Heaven within me glows! Here in my heart a flame is brightly burning, burning with love that only God bestows!	Wie wär' ich kalt, mich glücklich nur zu nennen, besitz' ich aller Himmel Seligkeit! Fühl' ich zu dir so süss mein Herz entbrennen, athme ich Wonnen, die nur Gott verleiht!

LOHENGRIN
(ardently)

If you, beloved, tell me you're contented, then all the joy of Heaven within me glows!	Vermagst du, Holde, glücklich dich zu nennen, giebst du auch mir des Himmels Seligkeit!

(tenderly)

Here in my heart a flame is brightly burning, burning with love that God alone bestows. I know that we are meant to be together! We had not met but sensed each other near; and then when I was chosen as your champion, I saw the way that love had paved was clear. You looked at me with eyes so bright and true, I knew at once that I would fight for you.	[25] Fühl' ich zu dir so süss mein Herz entbrennen, athme ich Wonnen, die nur Gott verleiht. Wie hehr erkenn' ich uns'rer Liebe Wesen! Die nie sich sah'n, wir hatten uns geahnt: war ich zu deinem Streiter auserlesen, hat Liebe mir zu dir den Weg gebahnt. Dein Auge sagte mir dich rein von Schuld, mich zwang dein Blick zu dienen deiner Huld.

ELSA

But long before I had already seen you, for in my dreams your image held me charmed:	Doch ich zuvor schon hatte dich gesehen, in sel'gem Traume warst du mir genaht:

and when I saw you here standing before me,	als ich nun wachend dich sah vor mir stehen,
I knew then you were sent at God's command.	erkannt' ich, dass du kamst auf Gottes Rath.
At once I longed to be within your power,	Da wollte ich vor deinem Blick zerfliessen,
and like a stream to wind around your feet,	gleich einem Bach umwinden deinen Schritt,
enchant your senses like a fragrant flower.	gleich einer Blume, duftend auf der Wiesen,
I was enslaved, my rapture was complete.	wollt' ich entzückt mich beugen deinem Tritt.
Can this be love? Where am I to find it,	Ist diess nur Liebe? Wie soll ich es nennen,
the word that will describe this joy divine?	diess Wort, so unaussprechlich wonnewoll,
Alas! your name, I must never know it,	wie, ach! dein Name, den ich nie soll kennen,
the name that would describe this love of mine!	bei dem ich nie mein Höchstes nennen soll!

LOHENGRIN
(caressingly)

Elsa!	Elsa!

ELSA

How sweet my name is when your lips reveal it.	Wie süss mein Name deinem Mund' entgleitet:

(somewhat hesitantly)

Why is the sweeter sound of yours denied?	Gönnst du des deinen holden Klang mir nicht?
But surely you no longer need conceal it now we are hidden from the world outside?	Nur, wenn zur Liebesstille wir geleitet, sollst du gestatten, dass mein Mund ihn spricht.

LOHENGRIN

My darling wife!	Mein süsses Weib!

ELSA

Whisper! They're all asleep.	Einsam, wenn Niemand wacht;
Yours is a secret I will always keep.	nie sei der Welt er zu Gehör gebracht!

Lohengrin takes Elsa in his gentle embrace and points through the open window to the flower-filled garden outside.

LOHENGRIN

Come, won't you share the night's mysterious perfumes?	[26] Athmest du nicht mit mir die süssen Düfte?
Where they are wafted from we'll never tell!	O wie so hold berauschen sie den Sinn!
A gentle breeze has brought them to your window:	Geheimnissvoll sie nahen durch die Lüfte,
gladly I shall surrender to their spell.	fraglos geb' ihrem Zauber ich mich hin.

(more forcefully)

Such is the magic spell that binds me to you.	So ist der Zauber, der mich dir verbunden,
Never did I need to know from whence you came;	da als ich zuerst, du Süsse, dich ersah;
I saw you there and from that moment loved you,	nicht deine Art ich brauchte zu erkunden,
with that one glance my heart was set aflame.	dich sah mein Aug' — mein Herz begriff dich da.
Just as these blissful perfumes have bewitched me,	Wie mir die Düfte hold den Sinn berücken,
though their mysterious source remains confused,	nah'n sie mir gleich aus räthselvoller Nacht:

so did your trust and innocence enchant me,	so deine Reine musste mich entzücken,
in spite of the crime of which you were accused.	traf ich dich auch in schwerer Schuld Verdacht.

Elsa conceals her mortification by nestling closer to Lohengrin in a gesture of submissiveness.

ELSA

Ah! Would that I could feel more worthy!	Ach! Könnt' ich deiner werth erscheinen!
Would I could be your saviour too!	Müsst' ich vor dir nicht bloss vergeh'n!
Gladly I'd offer my protection,	Könnt' ein Verdienst mich dir vereinen,
willingly suffer pain for you!	dürft' ich in Pein für dich mich seh'n!
I called to you in desperation.	Wie du mich trafst vor schwerer Klage,
Oh, would that you had summoned me!	o! wüsste ich auch dich in Noth!
If you faced even mortal danger	Dass muthvoll ich ein Mühen trage,
I'd be the first to set you free!	kennt' ich ein Sorgen, das dir droht!
What is the reason for your secret?	Wär' das Geheimniss so geartet,
Why must it always be concealed?	das aller Welt verschweigt dein Mund?

(increasingly mysteriously)

Perhaps disaster may await you	Vielleicht, dass Unheil dich erwartet,
if it should ever be revealed?	würd' aller Welt es offen kund?
If that's so, you still can tell me,	Wär' es so, und dürft' ich's wissen,
all knowledge of it I'd deny.	dürft' ich in meiner Macht es seh'n,
No force could ever wrench it from me,	durch Keines Droh'n sei mir's entrissen,
for you I'd be prepared to die!	für dich wollt' ich zum Tode geh'n!

LOHENGRIN

Beloved!	Geliebte!

ELSA
(more and more passionately)

Oh, make me proud because you trust me,	O mach' mich stolz durch dein Vertrauen,
proud of the faith in me you show!	dass ich in Unwerth nicht vergeh'!
You must believe I'd keep the secret.	Lass dein Geheimniss mich durchschauen,

(slowly)

Yes, who you are, I have to know!	dass, wer du bist, ich offen seh'!

LOHENGRIN

Be silent, Elsa!	Ach, schweige, Elsa!

ELSA
(more and more insistently)

If you love me, reveal what I've a right to share!	Meiner Treue enthülle deines Adels Werth!
If you will say where you have come from,	Woher du kamst, sag' ohne Reue:
an oath of silence I shall swear!	durch mich sei Schweigens Kraft bewährt!

LOHENGRIN
(sternly and earnestly stepping back a few paces)

Can you forget the trust that I have shown you?	Höchstes Vertrau'n hast du mir schon zu danken,
Did I not trust the solemn oath you made?	da deinem Schwur ich Glauben gern gewährt;
If from now on you never break the promise,	wirst nimmer du vor dem Gebote wanken,
I swear to you our love will never fade!	hoch über alle Frau'n dünkst du mich werth!

(He quickly and fondly turns back to Elsa once more.)

Come here to me, my love, my Elsa!
Come closer, to my burning heart!
Allow those eyes to shine upon me!
In their soft light my cares depart!

(ardently)

Oh, let these loving arms enfold you!
In them may all your troubles cease!
Ah, let me now and always hold you!
In you I find my joy and peace!
Your love shall be the consolation
for all that I have left behind;
for you I left a life more noble
than any other man could find.
Monarchs could offer me their
  kingdoms,
I would be happy to refuse.
My Elsa's love alone consoles me
for every blessing that I lose!
So cast away your doubts for ever,
my sacrifice has cost me dear.
I did not come from night and sadness:

from light and joy I journeyed here!

An meine Brust, du Süsse, Reine!
Sei meines Herzens Glühen nah',
dass mich dein Auge sanft bescheine,
in dem ich all' mein Glück ersah!

O, gönne mir, dass mit Entzücken
ich deinen Athem sauge ein!
Lass fest, ach! fest an mich dich drücken,
dass ich in dir mög' glücklich sein!
Dein Lieben muss mir hoch entgelten
für das, was ich um dich verliess;
kein Loos in Gottes weiten Welten
wohl edler als das meine hiess'.
Böt' mir der König seine Krone,

ich dürfte sie mit Recht verschmäh'n:
das einz'ge, was mein Opfer lohne,
muss ich in deiner Lieb' erseh'n!
Drum wolle stets den Zweifel meiden,
dein Lieben sei mein stolz Gewähr;
denn nicht komm' ich aus Nacht und
  Leiden,
aus Glanz und Wonne kam ich her.

ELSA

O God! Can I believe this?
You mean what you have said?
You try to reassure me,
but bring me grief instead!
The life you have abandoned
is that for which you yearn.
You came to me from Heaven:
you're longing to return!
My pitiful devotion
will never be enough.
I know that I shall lose you
when you regret your love.

Hilf Gott! Was muss ich hören!
Welch' Zeugniss gab dein Mund!
Du wolltest mich bethören, -
nun wird mir Jammer kund!
Das Loos, dem du entronnen,
es war dein höchstes Glück:
du kamst zu mir aus Wonnen,
und sehnest dich zurück!
Wie soll ich Ärmste glauben,
dir g'nüge meine Treu'?
Ein Tag wird dich mir rauben
durch deiner Liebe Reu'!

LOHENGRIN

Now stop all this self-torture!

Halt' ein, dich so zu quälen!

ELSA

Why do you torment me?
Am I to count the hours
till you decide to leave?
This terrible foreboding
will make me pale and wan.
Away from me you'll hasten:
I'll wake and find you gone!

Was quälest du mich doch!
Soll ich die Tage zählen,
die du mir bleibest noch?
In Sorg' um dein Verweilen
verblüht die Wange mir;
dann wirst du mir enteilen,
im Elend bleib' ich hier!

LOHENGRIN
(animatedly)

Never will you beauty vanish
while you are free from doubt.

Nie soll dein Reiz entschwinden,
bleibst du von Zweifel rein.

ELSA

Ah! Must I lose the saviour
I cannot live without?
By magic you were brought here,
by sorcery bizarre.
I never shall be happy
not knowing who you are!
Ah! What was that? There's
something, did you hear it?

Ach! Dich an mich zu binden,
wie sollt' ich mächtig sein?
Voll Zauber ist dein Wesen,
durch Wunder kamst du her:
wie sollt' ich da genesen?
wo fänd' ich dein Gewähr?
Hörtest du nichts? Vernahmest du kein
Kommen?

She starts up in the most violent agitation and pauses in order to listen.

LOHENGRIN

Elsa!   Elsa!

ELSA .
(staring ahead)

Ah no! Look there — the swan! The swan!	Ach nein! — Doch dort! Der Schwan, der Schwan!
He's gliding here across the silent water . . .	Dort kommt er auf der Wasserfluth geschwommen . . .
You've summoned him, he's coming to the shore!	Du rufest ihm, — er zieht herbei den Kahn!

LOHENGRIN

Elsa, be still! Upset yourself no more!	Elsa, halt' ein! Beruh'ge deinen Wahn!

ELSA

I cannot quell this madness,	Nichts kann mir Ruhe geben,
I never shall be calm.	dem Wahn mich nichts entreisst,
Yes, even if it kills me,	als — gelt' es auch mein Leben!
I must know who you are!	zu wissen — wer du sei'st?

LOHENGRIN

Elsa, you cannot mean this!	Elsa, was willst du wagen?

ELSA

You poor ill-fated man,	Unselig holder Mann,
I have to ask the questions!	hör', was ich dich muss fragen:
Say who your father is!	Den Namen sag' mir an!

LOHENGRIN

Enough!	Halt' ein!

ELSA

From whence you came?	Woher die Fahrt?

LOHENGRIN

Stop this!	Weh' dir!

ELSA

What is your name?	Wie deine Art?

LOHENGRIN

Elsa! What have you done?	Weh' uns, was thatest du!

She suddenly notices Frederick and his four companions breaking in through one of the doors at the back with their swords drawn.

ELSA
(with a scream)

Save yourself! Your sword, your sword!	Rette dich! Dein Schwert! Dein Schwert!

She quickly hands Lohengrin his sword, which had been resting against the couch, so that he is able to draw it swiftly from its scabbard, which she continues to hold. As Frederick raises his arm to strike, Lohengrin strikes him dead with a single blow; the swords fall from the hands of the terrified nobles, who throw themselves on their knees at Lohengrin's feet. Elsa, who had thrown herself upon Lohengrin's breast, sinks slowly to the ground in a faint. Long silence. Deeply shaken, Lohengrin alone remains standing.

LOHENGRIN

Now and for ever our joy is gone!	Weh'! Nun ist all' unser Glück dahin!

He bends down to Elsa, gently lifts her up and places her on the couch.

ELSA
(weakly opening her eyes)

Almighty one, oh, pity me!   Allewiger! Erbarm' dich mein!

At a sign from Lohengrin, the four nobles rise to their feet.

LOHENGRIN

Carry the body to be judged by the King!   Tragt den Erschlag'nen vor des König's
            Gericht!

*The four nobles take up Frederick's body and bear it away through the door on the right. Lohengrin
rings a bell: two women enter from the left.*

Take my sweet Elsa and prepare her.   Sie vor den König zu geleiten,
Before the King she shall appear.   schmückt Elsa, meine süsse Frau!
There I shall answer all her questions,   Dort will ich Antwort ihr bereiten,
and who I am shall then be clear.   dass die des Gatten Art erschau'.

*He leaves with a sadly solemn demeanour. The women lead Elsa away to the left: she is incapable
of uttering a single word. Day has slowly begun to dawn; the candles have gone out. A large
curtain is drawn across the front of the stage, closing off the whole area behind it.*

Scene Three. *When the downstage curtain opens again, the scene represents the meadow on
the banks of the Scheldt, as in the first act; a brilliant red sky; it gradually becomes fully light. A
count enters downstage right with his army of followers and, dismounting, entrusts his horse to the
care of a squire. Two pages bring him his shield and spear. He plants his banner, around which
his followers assemble. A second count enters in the same manner as the first, while the trumpets
of a third can already be heard approaching. The third count now enters with his followers. The
new troops assemble under their respective banners; the counts and nobles greet each other,
examining and praising each others' weapons, and so on. A fourth count enters stage right with
his followers and takes up his position upstage centre. When the King's trumpeters are heard, all
hurry to group themselves under their banners. The King enters from the left with his Saxon militia.*

ALL THE MEN
(striking their shields as the King reaches the oak)

Hail, hail King Henry!   Heil König Heinrich!
Hail, King Henry, hail!   König Heinrich Heil!

KING HENRY

I thank you, people of Brabant!   Habt Dank, ihr Lieben von Brabant!
Proudly I see you gathered round.   Wie fühl' ich froh mein Herz entbrannt,
Would that throughout this glorious   find' ich in jedem deutschen Land
   land
such valiant men as you were found!   so kräftig reichen Heerverband!
Now let the Empire's foes attack,   Nun soll des Reiches Feind sich nah'n,
we are prepared to drive them back.   wir wollen tapfer ihn empfah'n:
Out from the East they'll ride in vain: aus seinem öden Ost daher
we will defeat them once again!   soll er sich nimmer wagen mehr!
Protect your country with your sword!   Für deutsches Land das deutsche
Triumph will be your just reward!   Schwert!
                     So sei des Reiches Kraft bewährt!

ALL THE MEN

Protect our land! Protect our sword!   Für deutsches Land das deutsche Schwert!
Triumph will be our just reward!   So sei des Reiches Kraft bewährt!

KING HENRY

Where is the man whom God has sent   Wo weilt nun der, den Gott gesandt
to guard the glory of Brabant?   zum Ruhm, zur Grösse von Brabant?

*Hesitant jostling among the crowd as the four nobles bring in Frederick's body on a bier and place
it in the centre of the circle.*

ALL THE MEN

What do they bear? What does this   Was bringen die? Was thun sie kund?
   mean?
These men are friends of Telramund.   Die Mannen sind's des Telramund.

KING HENRY

I fear the worst. Who have you brought?	Was führt ihr her? Was soll ich schau'n?
What dreadful news must you report?	Mich fasst bei eurem Anblick Grau'n!

FOUR NOBLES

Our new Protector sent us here; and who this is he will make clear.	So will's der Schützer von Brabant: wer dieser ist, macht er bekannt.

Elsa enters with a large retinue of women and advances with slow and tottering steps.

ALL THE MEN

Look, Elsa comes, the pure and virtuous!	Seht! Elsa naht, die tugendreiche:

(The King goes to meet Elsa and conducts her to a seat opposite the oak.)

Why is her face so pale and troubled?	wie ist ihr Antlitz trüb' und bleiche!

KING HENRY

Why do you seem so sad and grieved?	Wie muss ich dich so traurig seh'n!
Is it because your husband must leave?	Will dir so nah' die Trennung geh'n?

Elsa tries to look up at him but cannot. Much jostling at the back of the stage.

VOICES
(upstage)

Make way for the Protector of Brabant!	Macht Platz dem Helden von Brabant!

Lohengrin enters, armed as in the first act, and strides solemnly and gravely to the front.

ALL THE MEN

Hail! Hail Protector of Brabant!	Heil! Heil dem Helden von Brabant!

KING HENRY

Welcome among us, worthy knight! Here are the men you called to fight; they know that victory will be sure, with you to lead them into war.	Heil deinem Kommen, theurer Held! Die du so treulich riefst in's Feld, die harren dein in Streites Lust, von dir geführt, des Sieg's bewusst.

ALL THE MEN

We know that victory will be sure, with you to lead us into war.	Wir harren dein in Streites Lust, von dir geführt, des Sieg's bewusst.

LOHENGRIN

Your Royal Highness, I must tell you: these valiant men whom I have summoned I cannot lead them into war.	Mein Herr und König, lass dir melden: die ich berief, die kühnen Helden, zum Streit sie führen darf ich nicht!

All express the deepest dismay.

KING HENRY, MEN AND WOMEN

O God! What can he mean by this!	Hilf Gott! welch' hartes Wort er spricht!

LOHENGRIN

As your new leader I am not appearing.	Als Streitgenoss bin nicht ich euch gekommen,
As plaintiff I must now demand a hearing:	als Kläger sei ich jetzt von euch vernommen!

(He uncovers Frederick's body, from the sight of which all turn away in disgust.)
(solemnly standing in front of the body)

I ask you all to listen to these charges,	Zum ersten klage laut ich vor euch Allen,

(slowly)

that truth and justice may be found. At dead of night this man fiercely attacked me. Say, was I right to strike him down?	und frag' um Spruch nach Recht und Fug: da dieser Mann zur Nacht mich überfallen, sagt, ob ich ihn mit Recht erschlug?

88

KING HENRY AND ALL THE MEN
(solemnly stretching out their hands towards the body)

As you have struck him down in this life, so God will punish him hereafter!	Wie deine Hand ihn schlug auf Erden, soll dort ihm Gottes Strafe werden!

LOHENGRIN

And now I bring another charge before you: before the world it must be made. The woman God has given me in marriage - my wife - by her am I betrayed!	Zum and'ren aber sollt ihr Klage hören: denn aller Welt nun klag' ich laut, dass zum Verrath an mir sich liess bethören das Weib, das Gott mir angetraut.

WOMEN
(looking at Elsa with reproachful gestures)

Shame on you! Elsa!	Wehe dir! Elsa!

KING HENRY AND ALL THE MEN
(deeply shocked and troubled)

Elsa! Oh, how can this be true? How could you do this dreadful thing?	Elsa! Wie mochte das gescheh'n? Wie konntest so du dich vergeh'n?

LOHENGRIN
(still very sternly)

You all remember how she gave her promise	Ihr hörtet Alle, wie sie mir versprochen,

(slowly)

that she would never ask me who I am. Now all the solemn vows she made are broken, now it is clear that they were all a sham.	dass nie sie woll' erfragen, wer ich bin? Nun hat sie ihren theuren Schwur gebrochen, treulosem Rath gab sie ihr Herz dahin!

(All express the most extreme dismay.)

To silence all the doubts that caused her anguish, I will reveal the secret that I hold: though I refused my enemies an answer, the truth of who I am must now be told.	Zu lohnen ihres Zweifels wildem Fragen, sei nun die Antwort länger nicht gespart: des Feindes Drängen durft' ich sie versagen, nun muss ich künden wie mein Nam' und Art.

(with an increasingly transfigured expression)

And you decide if I should shun the daylight! Before the world, and here before your King I will reveal the secret that surrounds me.	Nun merket wohl, ob ich den Tag muss scheuen: vor aller Welt, vor König und vor Reich enthülle mein Geheimniss ich in Treuen.

(raising himself to his full height)

So judge if I am worthy of your trust!	Nun hört, ob ich an Adel euch nicht gleich!

KING HENRY AND ALL THE MEN

She asked the question which he had forbidden! Oh, would she had let him keep his secret hidden!	Welch' Unerhörtes muss ich nun erfahren; O könnt' er die erzwung'ne Kunde sich ersparen!

LOHENGRIN

There is a land beyond the realm of mortals, where there's a castle, Monsalvat its name; a shining temple lies within its portals, more radiant than any place of earthly fame.	In fernem Land, unnahbar euren Schritten, liegt eine Burg, die Monsalvat genannt; ein lichter Tempel stehet dort in Mitten, so kostbar, als auf Erden nichts bekannt:

It holds a vessel of the purest beauty

that represents the heights of sacred
love.
That virtuous men might guard it as
their duty
a host of angels brought it from above.
Once every year a dove descends from
Heaven
to fortify anew its wondrous grace.
The Holy Grail, it grants its faith for
ever
unto the brotherhood within that place.
The knight the Grail has chosen as its
servant
is blest with its divine celestial might;
by him all evil men will be defeated,
and death itself grows pale and takes to
flight.
When he is summoned to a distant
country
to fight the cause of virtue in the field,
all the power of the Grail will not desert
him
if his identity remains concealed.
For so sublime is its most sacred
blessing,
if ever it's revealed, it hides from view,
and that is why the knight must not be
doubted,
for if he is, he may not stay with you.

And now I answer the forbidden
questions:
the Grail sent me, from Monsalvat I
came;
my father Parsifal leads us in glory;
I am his knight, and Lohengrin my name.

drinn ein Gefäss von wunderthät'gem
Segen
wird dort als höchstes Heiligthum
bewacht,
es ward, dass sein der Menschen
reinste pflegen,
herab von einer Engelschaar gebracht;
alljährlich naht vom Himmel eine
Taube,
um neu zu stärken seine Wunderkraft:
es heisst der Gral, und selig reinster
Glaube
ertheilt durch ihn sich seiner Ritterschaft.
Wer nun dem Gral zu dienen ist
erkoren,
den rüstet er mit überirdischer Macht;
an dem ist jedes Bösen Trug verloren,
wenn ihn er ersieht, weicht dem des
Todes Nacht.
Selbst wer von ihm in ferne Land'
entsendet,
zum Streiter für der Tugend Recht ernannt,
dem wird nicht seine heil'ge Kraft
entwendet,
bleibt als sein Ritter dort er unerkannt:
so hehrer Art doch ist des Grales Segen,

enthüllt - muss er des Laien Auge flieh'n;
des Ritters drum sollt Zweifel ihr nicht
hegen,
erkennt ihr ihn, dann muss er von euch
zieh'n.

Nun hört, wie ich verbot'ner Frage
lohne!
Vom Gral ward ich zu euch daher
gesandt:
mein Vater Parzival trägt seine Krone,
sein Ritter ich — bin Lohengrin genannt.

KING HENRY, ALL THE MEN AND WOMEN
(deeply moved)

Ah! To think that he came to us from
Heaven!
My eyes are filled with tears of adoration.

Hör' ich so seine höchste Art bewähren,

entbrennt mein Aug' in heil'gen
Wonnezähren.

ELSA

The earth is shaking! I can't breathe!

It's dark! Ah! I've been so foolish!

Mir schwankt der Boden! Welche
Nacht!
O Luft! Luft der Unglücksel'gen!

She is on the verge of collapse; Lohengrin catches her in his arms.

LOHENGRIN

O Elsa! Why have you done this to me?
Ah! I remember when I saw you first,
my heart then overflowed with love for
you.
That moment life began for me anew.

My wondrous power, the secret of the
Grail,
the knowledge that my strength would
never fail -
all this I longed to offer with my heart.

O Elsa! Was hast du mir angethan?
Als meine Augen dich zuerst ersah'n,
zu dir fühlt' ich in Liebe mich entbrannt,

und schnell hatt' ich ein neues Glück
erkannt:
die hehre Macht, die Wunder meiner
Art,
die Kraft, die mein Geheimniss mir
bewahrt,
wollt' ich dem Dienst des reinsten
Herzens weih'n:

Why did you force me to reveal my name?
Now I must leave! We'll never meet again!

was rissest du nun mein Geheimniss ein?
Jetzt muss ich, ach! von dir geschieden sein!

KING HENRY, ALL THE MEN AND WOMEN

What sorrow! Must you leave us now?
You noble hero sent from God!
If God protects our land no more,
who will defend us all in war?

Weh'! Wehe! Musst du von uns zieh'n?
Du hehrer, gottgesandter Mann!
Soll uns des Himmels Segen flieh'n,
wo fänden dein wir Tröstung dann?

ELSA
(starting up in utter despair)

My husband! No! I cannot let you leave me!
I'll show that I'm repentant! Stay with me!
You can't ignore my great remorse and sorrow!
I fall before you: punish me, I beg you!

Mein Gatte, nein! Ich lass' dich nicht von hinnen!
Als Zeuge meiner Busse bleibe hier!
Nicht darfst du meiner bittern Reu' entrinnen;
dass du mich strafest liege ich vor dir!

LOHENGRIN

I have no choice, my lovely wife!
The Grail has called: I must obey at once!

Ich muss, ich muss, mein süsses Weib!
Schon zürnt der Gral, dass ich ihm ferne bleib'!

ELSA

If you are truly sent at God's command,
do not deny the mercy He can grant!
I shall repent my crime throughout my life.
Ah! Stay to comfort your remorseful wife!
Reject me not, I know how I have failed you!

Bist du so göttlich, als ich dich erkannt,
sei Gottes Gnade nicht aus dir verbannt!
Büsst sie in Jammer ihre schwere Schuld,
nicht flieh' die Ärmste deiner Nähe Huld!
Verstoss' mich nicht, wie gross auch mein Verbrechen!

LOHENGRIN

There's one atonement, penance for your crime!
Ah! I as you suffer this cruel pain!
We must be parted! You must understand:
this the atonement, this the Grail's command!

Nur eine Strafe giebt's für dein Vergeh'n,
ach, mich wie dich trifft ihre herbe Pein!
Getrennt, geschieden sollen wir uns seh'n,
diess muss die Strafe, diess die Sühne sein!

Elsa sinks back with a cry.

KING HENRY AND ALL THE MEN
(impetuously crowding around Lohengrin)

O stay! You cannot ever leave us!

Your men are waiting for their leader.

O bleib', und zieh' uns nicht von dannen!

Des Führers harren deine Mannen.

LOHENGRIN

I cannot stay! I cannot lead your army!

O König, hör'! Ich darf dich nicht geleiten!

(animatedly and quickly)

Once he's discovered, the knight of the Grail
would disobey if he went into battle.
He'd have no human strength with which to fight.
But, great King Henry, I know that in the future
a great and glorious war awaits these men.

Des Grales Ritter, habt ihr ihn erkannt,
wollt' er in Ungehorsam mit euch streiten,
ihm wäre alle Manneskraft entwandt!
Doch, grosser König, lass mich dir weissagen:
dir Reinem ist ein grosser Sieg verlieh'n.

And from that victory for ever after

the Eastern hordes won't threaten you
again.

Nach Deutschland sollen noch in
fernsten Tagen
des Ostens Horden siegreich niemals
zieh'n!

Lively excitement.

MEN AND WOMEN

The swan! The swan!
Look there, it has returned!

Der Schwan! Der Schwan!
Seht dort ihn wieder nah'n!

At this point the swan passes the bend in the river, drawing the empty skiff. Recovering from her torpor, Elsa raises herself in her seat and looks towards the river bank.

ELSA

How dreadful! Ah! The swan!

Entsetzlich! Ha, der Schwan!

She remains in her present position for a long time, as though petrified.

LOHENGRIN
(shaken)

The prodigal is summoned by the Grail.

Schon sendet nach dem Säumigen der
Gral.

(Amidst the keenest expectancy on the part of all the bystanders, Lohengrin approaches the water's edge and bends over the swan, gazing at it sadly.)

Beloved swan!
Ah! How I wish you could be spared
this last distressing journey here!
In just one year you'd have been free,
your term of duty at an end!
Freed by the Grail, you would appear
back to your human form again.

Mein lieber Schwan!
Ach, diese letzte, traur'ge Fahrt,
wie gern hätt' ich sie dir erspart!
In einem Jahr, wenn deine Zeit
im Dienst zu Ende sollte geh'n,
dann durch des Grales Macht befreit,
wollt' ich dich anders wieder seh'n!

(He turns back downstage towards Elsa in violent anguish.)

O Elsa! If we had one year together,
all of our sorrows would be joys instead!

O Elsa! Nur ein Jahr an deiner Seite
hätt' ich als Zeuge deines Glück's
ersehnt!

Then by the Grail you'd have been
reunited
with your brother Godfrey, whom you
thought was dead.

Dann kehrte, selig in des Grals Geleite,
dein Bruder wieder, den du todt
gewähnt.

(All express their great surprise.)
(handing his horn, sword and ring to Elsa)

Since he'll return when I'm no longer
with you,
this horn, this sword, this ring for him I
give you.
The horn will protect him when in
danger,
the sword will bring him victory and
fame;
and with the ring remind him how a
stranger
had set you free from misery and shame.

Kommt er dann heim, wenn ich ihm fern
im Leben,
diess Horn, diess Schwert, den Ring
sollst du ihm geben.
Diess Horn soll in Gefahr ihm Hülfe
schenken,
in wildem Kampf diess Schwert ihm Sieg
verleiht:
doch bei dem Ringe soll er mein
gedenken,
der einst auch dich aus Schmach und
Noth befreit!

(repeatedly kissing Elsa, who is no longer capable of any expression)

Farewell! Farewell! Farewell! My lovely
wife!
Farewell! The Grail has called, I must
obey.

Leb' wohl! Leb' wohl! Leb' wohl, mein
süsses Weib!
Leb' wohl! Mein zürnt der Gral, wenn
ich noch bleib'!

He hurries quickly to the river bank.

KING HENRY, MEN AND WOMEN

Stay! Stay, you noble, blessed man!
We beg you don't abandon us!

Weh', weh'! Du edler, holder Mann!
Welch' harte Noth thust du uns an!

(suddenly appearing at the front of the stage)

Go home! Go home, you stubborn
  hero,
that I may tell your foolish Elsa
who draws the boat you ride upon!
I placed that chain around his neck.
He may appear to be a swan,
but he's the rightful Duke of Brabant!

Fahr' heim! Fahr' heim, du stolzer
  Helde,
dass jubelnd ich der Thörin melde,
wer dich gezogen in dem Kahn!
Am Kettlein, das ich um ihn wand,
ersah ich wohl, wer dieser Schwan:
es ist der Erbe von Brabant!

ALL

Ah!

Ha!

ORTRUD
(to Elsa)

Thank you for driving out your saviour!
Now watch them disappear from view!
For if the knight had stayed for longer,
he would have freed your brother too.

Dank, dass den Ritter du vertrieben!
Nun giebt der Schwan ihm Heimgeleit:
der Held, wär' länger er geblieben,
den Bruder hätt' er auch befreit.

ALL
(in extreme indignation)

You have confessed! Ah! Hateful
  woman!
So you've confessed your dreadful
  crime!

Abscheulich Weib! Ha, welch'
  Verbrechen
hast du in frechem Hohn bekannt!

ORTRUD

But learn, see how the gods have
  vengeance
on those who turn from them in scorn!

Erfahrt, wie sich die Götter rächen,

von deren Huld ihr euch gewandt!

Drawing herself up to her full height, she remains standing in a state of of wild delirium. Lohengrin, who has already reached the water's edge, has been listening attentively to Ortrud and now sinks to his knees in silent prayer. All eyes are turned on him in intense expectancy. The white dove of the Grail hovers over the skiff. Lohengrin sees it and, with a look of gratitude, leaps up and loosens the chain from the swan's neck, whereupon the swan immediately disappears beneath the waves. In its place Lohengrin lifts up a handsome boy in a glittering silver garment (Godfrey) and sets him down on the bank.

LOHENGRIN

Behold the ruler of Brabant!
Your rightful leader has returned!

Seht da den Herzog von Brabant!
Zum Führer sei er euch ernannt!

On seeing Godfrey, Ortrud collapses with a scream. Lohengrin leaps quickly into the skiff, which the dove, seizing the chain, now draws away. Elsa gazes at Godfrey with an expression of ultimate joyful transfiguration as he comes forward and makes his obeisance to the King: all look at him in blissful astonishment, while the Brabantine nobles sink down on their knees in homage to him. Godfrey runs to embrace Elsa; after a brief moment of rapturous joy, she turns swiftly to the shore, but Lohengrin is no longer to be seen.

ELSA

My husband! My husband!

Mein Gatte! Mein Gatte!

(Lohengrin again becomes visible in the distance. He is standing in the skiff, head bowed, leaning sadly on his shield; on seeing him, all break into a loud cry of anguish.)

Ah!

Ah!

She sinks lifeless to the ground in Godfrey's arms.

KING HENRY, MEN AND WOMEN

Ah!

Weh'!

As Lohengrin gradually vanishes from sight, the curtain slowly falls.

Scenes from the 1987 Bayreuth production by Werner Herzog and Henning von Gierke, with Catarina Ligendza as Elsa, Paul Frey as Lohengrin and Gabriele Schnaut as Ortrud (photo: Rauh)

Select Bibliography

Stewart Spencer

Wagner's own comments on Lohengrin may be found in his autobiography *My Life* (Cambridge 1983) and his 1851 essay *A Communication to my Friends* (available only in William Ashton Ellis's translation: *Richard Wagner's Prose Works* [London 1892-99], I, 267-392), although both these sources need to be treated circumspectly, since Wagner is guilty here of rewriting the past in the light of his current thinking.

The best introductions to the opera may be found in Ernest Newman's *Wagner Nights* (first published in 1949 and rarely out of print since then), Carl Dahlhaus's *Richard Wagner's Music Dramas* (Cambridge 1979) and Barry Millington's *Wagner* (a second edition of which appeared in paperback in 1992). Wagnerians with a reading knowledge of German and French may find much of interest in single-volume introductions to the opera published by rororo opernb•ücher (Reinbek 1989) and L'Avant-Scène Opéra (Paris 1992) respectively. Wagner's prose draft was published for the first time in the Bayreuther Festspielführer for 1936, pp. 143-70; an English translation appeared in *Wagner*, iv (1983), 34-49. The musical sketches are discussed by John Deathridge in 'Through the Looking Glass: Some Remarks on the First Complete Draft of *Lohengrin*', *Analysing Opera: Verdi and Wagner*, ed. Carolyn Abbate and Roger Parker (Berkeley 1989), 56-92. In general, however, the opera has received little critical attention, although no bibliography would be complete without at least a mention of Charles Baudelaire, 'Richard Wagner et *Tannhäuser* à Paris' (Paris 1861); English trans., 1964; Helen M. Mustard and Charles E. Passage (trans.), Wolfram von Eschenbach: *Parzival* (New York 1961); Christopher McIntosh, *The Swan King: Ludwig II of Bavaria* (London 1982); Oswald Georg Bauer, Richard Wagner: *The Stage Designs and Productions from the Premières to the Present* (New York 1983); and Thomas Mann, *Pro and Contra Wagner* (London 1985).

For the mythical and historical background readers will find the following of interest: Marina Warner *Alone of All Her Sex. The Myth and the Cult of the Virgin Mary* (London, 1976; 1985); Georges Duby *The Knight, the Lady and the Priest* (London, 1984); C. Brooke *The Medieval Idea of Marriage* (Oxford, 1991); J. B. Gillingham 'Love, marriage and politics in the twelfth century' *Forum for Modern Language Studies* 25 (1989); J. Martindale 'Succession and politics in the Romance-speaking world c.1000 - 1140' in *England and her Neighbours*, ed. M. Jones and M. Vale (London, 1989); Volker Mertens 'Wagner's Middle Ages' in the *Wagner Handbook* ed. U. Müller and P. Wapnewski, trans. Deathridge (Harvard, 1992) and L. Harf-Lancner *Les Fées au moyen âge: Mõrgane et Mélusine/ La naissance des fées* (Paris, 1987).

Contributors

John Deathridge is a Fellow of King's College Cambridge and the editor of the critical edition of the *Lohengrin* score.

Thomas S. Grey is Assistant Professor at Stanford University, California.

Janet L. Nelson is Professor of Medieval History at King's College London and a co-convenor of the Women's History Seminar at the Institute of Historical Research, University of London. She is the author of *Ritual and Politics in Early Medieval Europe* (1986) and *Charles the Bold* (1992).

Stewart Spencer is the editor of *Wagner* Magazine and co-editor of *Selected Letters of Richard Wagner* and *Wagner in Performance*.

Amanda Holden is General Editor of *The Viking Opera Guide* (London, 1993), and the translator of many operas including *Ariodante, The Marriage of Figaro, La bohème* and *Les Boréades*.

Discography

This list includes the live and studio recordings of *Lohengrin* currently available, given in chronological order. There are at present only three studio recordings, and experts disagree as to their relative merits.

F. Völker (*Lohengrin*), M. Müller (*Elsa*), M. Klose (*Ortrud*), J. Prohaska (*Telramund*), L. Hofmann (*King Henry*), W. Grossmann (*Herald*). Berlin State Opera Chorus and Orchestra / R. Heger
Preiser 90043 (3 CDs). Live recording, 1942; CD release, 1992

L. Melchior (*L*), A. Varnay (*E*), K. Thorborg (*O*), A. Sved (*T*), N. Cordon (*KH*), M. Harrell (*H*). Metropolitan Opera Chorus and Orchestra, New York / E. Leinsdorf
Myto 3MDC 924.66 (3 CDs). Live recording, 1943

W. Windgassen (*L*), B. Nilsson (*E*), A. Varnay (*O*), H. Uhde (*T*), T. Adam (*KH*), D. Fischer-Dieskau (*H*). Bayreuth Festival Chorus and Orchestra / E. Jochum
Arkadia 3CDMP 431 (3 CDs). Live recording, 1954; CD release, 1991

S. Kónya (*L*), L. Rysanek (*E*), A. Varnay (*O*), E. Blanc (*T*), K. Engen (*KH*), E. Wächter (*H*). Bayreuth Festival Chorus and Orchestra / A. Cluytens
Myto 3MDC 890.02 (3 CDs). Live recording, 1958; CD release, 1989

J. Thomas (*L*), E. Grümmer (*E*), C. Ludwig (*O*), D. Fischer-Dieskau (*T*), G. Frick (*KH*), O. Wiener (*H*). Vienna State Opera Chorus, Vienna Philharmonic Orchestra / R. Kempe
EMI CDS7 49017-8 (3 CDs). Original recording, 1964; CD release, 1988

J. Thomas (*L*), I. Bjoner (*E*), A. Varnay (*O*), G. Neidlinger (*T*), F. Crass (*KH*), T. Krause (*H*). Prague Philharmonic Chorus, Orchestra of La Scala, Milan / W. Sawallich
MEL 37067 (3 CDs). Live recording, 1965

R. Kollo (*L*), A. Tomowa-Sintow (*E*), D. Vejzovic (*O*), S. Nimsgern (*T*), K. Ridderbusch (*KH*), R. Kerns (*H*). Berlin Deutsche Opera Chorus, Berlin Philharmonic Orchestra / H. von Karajan
EMI CMS7 69314-2 (4 CDs). Original recording, 1972; CD release, 1988

P. Domingo (*L*), J. Norman (*E*), E. Randová (*O*), S. Nimsgern (*T*), H. Sotin (*KH*), D. Fischer-Dieskau (*H*). Vienna State Opera Concert Chorus, Vienna Philharmonic Orchestra / G. Solti
Decca 421 053-2DH4 (4 CDs). 1987

P. Frey (*L*), C. Studer (*E*), G. Schnaut (*O*), E. Wlaschiha (*T*), M. Schenk (*KH*), E. W. Schulte (*H*) Bayreuth Festival Chorus and Orchestra / P. Schneider
Philips 434 602-2PH4 (4 CDs). Live recording, 1990; CD release 1992

Video

P. Domingo (*L*), C. Studer (*E*), D. Vejzovic (*O*), H. Welker (*T*), R. Lloyd (*KH*), G. Tichy (*H*) Vienna State Opera Chorus and Orchestra / C. Abbado
Polygram VVD841 (VHS). 1990

P. Hofmann (*L*), K. Armstrong (*E*), E. Connell (*O*), L. Roar (*T*), S. Vogel (*KH*), B. Weikl (*H*). Bayreuth Festival Chorus and Orchestra / W. Nelsson
Philips 070 411-3PHG2 (VHS); 070 411-1PHG2 (Laser Disc).1991

P. Frey (*L*), C. Studer (*E*), G. Schnaut (*O*), E. Wlaschiha (*T*), M. Schenk (*KH*), E. W. Schulte (*H*). Bayreuth Festival Chorus and Orchestra / P. Schneider
Philips (VHS, Laser Disc). 1993